WITHDRAWN

Stories from the Greek Tragedians

By the
REV. ALFRED J. CHURCH, M.A.

AUTHOR OF

"Stories from Homer" and "Stories from Virgil"

New York
Dodd, Mead and Company
Publishers

To my Sons,

ALFRED, MAURICE, HERBERT,

RICHARD, EDWARD, HARALD,

This Book

IS DEDICATED.

CONTENTS.

	PAGE
THE STORY OF THE LOVE OF ALCESTIS,	1
THE STORY OF THE VENGEANCE OF MEDEA,	23
THE STORY OF THE DEATH OF HERCULES,	45
THE STORY OF THE SEVEN CHIEFS AGAINST THEBES,	63
THE STORY OF ANTIGONE,	80
THE STORY OF IPHIGENIA IN AULIS,	98
THE STORY OF PHILOCTETES, OR THE BOW OF HERCULES,	116
THE STORY OF THE DEATH OF AGAMEMNON,	139
THE STORY OF ELECTRA, OR THE RETURN OF ORESTES,	158
THE STORY OF THE FURIES, OR THE LOOSING OF ORESTES,	186
THE STORY OF IPHIGENIA AMONG THE TAURIANS,	198
THE STORY OF THE PERSIANS, OR THE BATTLE OF SALAMIS,	219
THE STORY OF ION,	237

THE STORY OF THE LOVE OF ALCESTIS.

Asclepius, the son of Apollo, being a mighty physician, raised men from the dead. But Zeus was wroth that a man should have such power, and so make of no effect the ordinance of the Gods. Wherefore he smote Asclepius with a thunderbolt and slew him. And when Apollo knew this, he slew the Cyclopés that had made the thunderbolts for his father Zeus, for men say that they make them on their forges that are in the mountain of Etna. But Zeus suffered not this deed to go unpunished, but passed this sentence on his son Apollo, that he should serve a mortal man for the space of a whole year. Wherefore, for all that he was a god, he kept the sheep of Admetus, who was the Prince of Pheræ in Thessaly. And Admetus knew not that he was a god; but, nevertheless, being a just man, dealt truly with him. And it came to pass after this that Admetus was sick unto death. But Apollo gained this grace for him of the Fates (which order of life and death for men), that he should live, if only he could find some one who should be willing to die in his stead. And he went to all his kinsmen and friends and asked this thing of them, but found no one that was willing so to die; only Alcestis his wife was willing.

And when the day was come on the which it was appointed for her to die, Death came that he might fetch her. And when he was come, he found Apollo walking to and fro before the palace of King Admetus, having his bow in his hand. And when Death saw him, he said—

"What doest thou here, Apollo? Is it not enough for thee to have kept Admetus from his doom? Dost thou keep watch and ward over this woman with thine arrows and thy bow?"

"Fear not," the god made answer, "I have justice on my side."

"If thou hast justice, what need of thy bow?"

"'Tis my wont to carry it."

"Ay, and it is thy wont to help this house beyond all right and law."

"Nay, but I was troubled at the sorrows of one that I loved, and helped him."

"I know thy cunning speech and fair ways; but this woman thou shalt not take from me."

"But consider; thou canst but have one life. Wilt thou not take another in her stead?"

"Her and no other will I have, for my honour is the greater when I take the young."

"I know thy temper, hated both of Gods and of men. But there cometh a guest to this house, whom Eurystheus sendeth to the snowy plains of Thrace, to fetch the horses of Lycurgus. Haply he shall persuade thee against thy will."

"Say what thou wilt; it shall avail nothing. And now I go to cut off a lock of her hair, for I take these firstfruits of them that die."

In the meantime, within the palace, Alcestis prepared herself for death. And first she washed her body with pure water from the river, and then she took from her coffer of cedar her fairest apparel, and adorned herself therewith. Then, being so arranged, she stood before the hearth and prayed, saying, "O Queen Heré, behold! I depart this day. Do thou therefore keep my children, giving to this one a noble husband and to that a loving wife." And all the altars that were in the house she visited in like manner, crowning them with myrtle leaves and praying at them. Nor did she weep at all, or groan, or grow pale. But at the last, when she came to her chamber, she cast herself upon the bed and kissed it, crying, " I hate thee not, though I die for thee, giving myself for my husband. And thee another wife shall possess, not more true than I am, but, maybe, more fortunate ! " And after she had left the chamber, she turned to it again and again with many tears. And all the while her children clung to her garments, and she took them up in her arms, the one first and then the other, and kissed them. And all the servants that were in the house bewailed their mistress, nor did she fail to reach her hand to each of them, greeting him. There was not one of them so vile but she spake to him and was spoken to again.

After this, when the hour was now come when she must die, she cried to her husband (for he held her in his arms, as if he would have stayed her that she should not depart), I see the boat of the dead, and Charon standing with his hand upon the pole, who calleth me, sa ing, ' Hasten ; thou delayest us;' and then again, ' A winged messenger of the dead looketh at me from under his dark eyebrows, and would lead me away. Dost thou not see him?'" Then after this she seemed now ready to die, yet again she gathered strength, and said to the King, " Listen, and I will tell thee before I die what I would have thee do. Thou knowest how I have given my life for thy life. For when I might have lived, and had for my husband any prince of Thessaly that I would- and dwelt here in wealth and royal state, yet could I not endure to be widowed of thee and that thy children should be fatherless. There, fore I spared not myself, though thy father and she that bare thee betrayed thee. But the Gods have ordered all this after their own pleasure. So be it. Do thou therefore make this recompense, which indeed thou owest to me, for what will not a man give for his life? Thou lovest these children even as I love them. Suffer them then to be rulers in this house, and bring not a step-mother over them who shall hate them and deal with them unkindly. A son, indeed, hath a tower of strength in his father. But, O my daughter, how shall it fare with thee, for thy mother will not give thee in marriage, nor be with thee, comforting thee in thy travail of children, when a mother most showeth kindness and love. And now farewell, for I die this day. And thou, too, farewell, my husband. Thou losest a true wife, and ye, too, my children, a true mother."

Then Admetus made answer, "Fear not, it shall be as thou wilt. I could not find other wife fair and well born and true as thou. Never more shall I gather revellers in my palace, or crown my head with garlands, or hearken to the voice of music. Never shall I touch the harp or sing to the Libyan flute. And some cunning craftsman shall make an image fashioned like unto thee, and this I will hold in my arms and think of thee. Cold comfort indeed, yet that shall ease somewhat of the burden of my soul. But oh! that I had the voice and melody of Orpheus, for then had I gone down to Hell and persuaded the Queen thereof or her husband with my song to let thee go; nor would the watch-dog of Pluto, nor Charon that ferrieth the dead, have hindered me but that I had brought thee to the light. But do thou wait for me there, for there will I dwell with thee; and when I die they shall lay me by thy side, for never was wife so true as thou."

Then said Alcestis, "Take these children as a gift from me, and be as a mother to them."

"O me!" he cried, "what shall I do, being bereaved of thee?"

And she said, "Time will comfort thee; the dead are as nothing."

But he said, "Nay, but let me depart with thee."

But the Queen made answer, "'Tis enough that I die in thy stead."

And when she had thus spoken she gave up the ghost.

Then the King said to the old men that were gathered together to comfort him, "I will see to this burial. And do ye sing a hymn as is meet to the god of the dead. And to all my people I make this decree: that they mourn for this woman, and clothe themselves in black, and shave their heads, and that such as have horses cut off their manes, and that there be not heard in the city the voice of the flute or the sound of the harp for the space of twelve months."

Then the old men sang the hymn as they had been bidden. And when they had finished, it befell that Hercules, who was on a journey, came to the palace and asked whether King Admetus was sojourning there.

And the old men answered, " 'Tis even so, Hercules. But what, I pray thee, bringeth thee to this land?"

"I am bound on an errand for King Eurystheus; even to bring back to him horses of King Diomed."

"How wilt thou do this? Dost thou not know this Diomed?"

"I know nought of him, nor of his land."

"Thou wilt not master him or his horses without blows."

"Even so, yet I may not refuse the tasks that are set to me."

"Thou art resolved then to do this thing or to die?"

"Ay; and this is not the first race that I have run."

"Thou wilt not easily bridle these horses."

"Why not? They breathe not fire from their nostrils."

"No, but they devour the flesh of men."

"What sayest thou? This is the food of wild beasts, not of horses."

"Yet 'tis true. Thou wilt see their mangers foul with blood."

"And the master of these steeds, whose son is he?"

"He is son of Ares, lord of the land of Thrace."

"Now this is a strange fate and a hard that maketh me fight ever with the sons of Ares, with Lycaon first, and with Cycnus next, and now with this King Diomed. But none shall ever see the son of Alcmena trembling before an enemy."

And now King Admetus came forth from the palace. And when the two had greeted one another, Hercules would fain know why the King had shaven his hair as one that mourned for the dead. And the King answered that he was about to bury that day one that was dear to him.

And when Hercules inquired yet further who this might be, the King said that his children were well, and his father also, and his mother. But of his wife he answered so that Hercules understood not that he spake of her. For he said that she was a stranger by blood, yet near in friendship, and that she had dwelt in his house, having been left an orphan of her father. Nevertheless Hercules would have departed and found entertainment elsewhere, for he would not be troublesome to his host. But the King suffered him not. And to the servant that stood by he said, " Take thou this guest to the guest-chamber ; and see that they that have charge of these matters set abundance of food before him. And take care that ye shut the doors between the chambers and the palace; for it is not meet that the guest at his meal should hear the cry of them that mourn."

And when the old men would know why the King, having so great a trouble upon him, yet entertained a guest, he made answer, " Would ye have commended me the more if I had caused him to depart from this house and this city? For my sorrow had not been one whit the less, and I had lost the praise of hospitality. And a right worthy host is he to me if ever I chance to visit the land of Argos."

And now they had finished all things for the burying of Alcestis, when the old man Pheres, the father of the King, approached, and servants came with him bearing robes and crowns and other adornments wherewith to do honour to the dead. And when he was come over against the bier whereon they had laid the dead woman, he spake to the King, saying, "I am come to mourn with thee, my son, for thou hast lost a noble wife. Only thou must endure, though this indeed is a hard thing. But take these adornments, for it is meet that she should be honoured who died for thee, and for me also, that I should not go down to the grave childless." And to the dead he said, "Fare thou well, noble wife, that hast kept this house from falling. May it be well with thee in the dwellings of the dead!"

But the King answered him in great wrath, "I did not bid thee to this burial, nor shall this dead woman be adorned with gifts of thine. Who art thou that thou shouldest bewail her? Surely thou art not father of mine. For being come to extreme old age, yet thou wouldst not die for thy son, but sufferedst this woman, being a stranger in blood, to die for me. Her therefore I count father and mother also. Yet this had been a noble deed for thee, seeing that the span of life that was left to thee was short. And I too had not been left to live out my days thus miserably, being bereaved of her whom I loved. Hast thou not had all happiness, thus having lived in kingly power from youth to age? And thou wouldst have left a son to come after thee, that thy house should not be spoiled by thine enemies. Have I not always done due reverence to thee and to my mother? And, lo! this is the recompense that ye make me. Wherefore I say to thee, make haste and raise other sons who may nourish thee in thy old age, and pay thee due honour when thou art dead, for I will not bury thee. To thee I am dead."

Then the old man spake, "Thinkest thou that thou art driving some Lydian and Phrygian slave that hath been bought with money, and forgettest that I am a freeborn man of Thessaly, as my father was freeborn before me? I reared thee to rule this house after me; but to die for thee, that I owed thee not. This is no custom among the Greeks that a father should die for his son. To thyself thou livest or diest. All that was thy due thou hast received of me; the kingdom over many people, and, in due time, broad lands which I also received of my father. How have I wronged thee? Of what have I defrauded thee? I ask thee not to die for me; and I die not for thee. Thou lovest to behold this light. Thinkest thou that thy father loveth it not? For the years of the dead are very long; but the days of the living are short yet sweet withal. But I say to thee that thou hast fled from thy fate in shameless fashion, and hast slain this woman. Yea, a woman hath vanquished thee, and yet thou chargest cowardice against me. In truth, 'tis a wise device of thine that thou mayest live for ever, if marrying many times, thou canst still persuade thy wife to die for thee. Be silent then, for shame's sake; and if thou lovest life, remember that others love it also."

So King Admetus and his father reproached each other with many unseemly words. And when the old man had departed, they carried forth Alcestis to her burial.

But when they that bare the body had departed, there came in the old man that had the charge of the guest-chambers, and spake, saying, "I have seen many guests that have come from all the lands under the sun to this palace of Admetus, but never have I given entertainment to such evil guest as this. For first, knowing that my lord was in sore trouble and sorrow, he forebore not to enter these gates. And then he took his entertainment in most unseemly fashion; for if he lacked aught he would call loudly for it; and then, taking a great cup wreathed with leaves of ivy in his hands, he drank great draughts of red wine untempered with water. And when the fire of the wine had warmed him, he crowned his head with myrtle boughs, and sang in the vilest fashion. Then might one hear two melodies, this fellow's songs, which he sang without thought for the troubles of my lord and the lamentation wherewith we servants lamented our mistress. But we suffered not this stranger to see our tears, for so my lord had commanded. Surely this is a grievous thing that I must entertain this stranger, who surely is some thief or robber.

And meanwhile they have taken my mistress to her grave, and I followed not after her, nor reached my hand to her, that was as a mother to all that dwell in this place."

When the man had so spoken, Hercules came forth from the guest-chamber, crowned with myrtle, having his face flushed with wine. And he cried to the servant, saying, " Ho, there! why lookest thou so solemn and full of care? Thou shouldst not scowl on thy guest after this fashion, being full of some sorrow that concerns thee not nearly. Come hither, and I will teach thee to be wiser. Knowest thou what manner of thing the life of a man is? I trow not. Hearken therefore. There is not a man who knoweth what a day may bring forth. Therefore I say to thee: Make glad thy heart; eat, drink, count the day that now is to be thine own, but all else to be doubtful. As for all other things, let them be, and hearken to my words. Put away this great grief that lieth upon thee, and enter into this chamber, and drink with me. Right soon shall the tinkling of the wine as it falleth into the cup ease thee of these gloomy thoughts. As thou art a man, be wise after the fashion of a man; for to them that are of a gloomy countenance, life, if only I judge rightly, is not life but trouble only."

Then the servant answered, "All this I know; but we have fared so ill in this house that mirth and laughter ill beseem us."

"But they tell me that this dead woman was a stranger. Why shouldst thou be so troubled, seeing that they who rule this house yet live."

"How sayest thou that they live? Thou knowest not what trouble we endure."

"I know it, unless thy lord strangely deceived me."

"My lord is given to hospitality."

"And should it hinder him that there is some stranger dead in the house?"

"A stranger, sayest thou? 'Tis passing strange to call her thus."

"Hath thy lord then suffered some sorrow that he told me not?"

"Even so, or I had not loathed to see thee at thy revels. Thou seest this shaven hair and these black robes."

"What then? who is dead? One of thy lord's children, or the old man his father?"

THE LOVE OF ALCESTIS.

"Stranger, 'tis the wife of Admetus that is dead."

"What sayest thou? And yet he gave me entertainment?"

"Yea, for he would not, for shame, turn thee from his house."

"O miserable man, what a helpmeet thou hast lost!"

"Ay, and we are all lost with her."

"Well I knew it; for I saw the tears in his eyes, and his head shaven, and his sorrowful regard; but he deceived me, saying that the dead woman was a stranger. Therefore did I enter the doors and make merry, and crown myself with garlands, not knowing what had befallen my host. But come, tell me; where doth he bury her? Where shall I find her?"

"Follow straight along the road that leadeth to Larissa, and thou wilt see her tomb in the outskirts of the city."

Then said Hercules to himself, "O my heart, thou hast dared many great deeds before this day; and now most of all must I show myself a true son of Zeus. Now will I save this dead woman Alcestis, and give her back to her husband, and make due recompense to Admetus. I will go, therefore, and watch for this black-robed king, even Death. Methinks I shall find him nigh unto the tomb, drinking the blood of the sacrifices. There will I lie in wait for him, and run upon him, and throw my arms about him, nor shall any one deliver him out of my hands, till he have given up to me this woman. But if it chance that I find him not there, and he come not to the feast of blood, I will go down to the Queen of Hell, to the land where the sun shineth not, and beg her of the Queen; and doubtless she will give her to me, that I may give her to her husband. For right nobly did he entertain me, and drave me not from his house, for all that he had been stricken by such sorrow. Is there a man in Thessaly, nay in the whole land of Greece, that is such a lover of hospitality? I trow not. Noble is he, and he shall know that he is no ill friend to whom he hath done this thing."

So he went his way. And when he was gone, Admetus came back from the burying of his wife, a great company following him, of whom the elders sought to comfort him in his sorrow.

And when he was come to the gates of his palace he cried, " How shall I enter thee? how shall I dwell in thee? Once I came within thy gates with many pine-torches from Pelion, and the merry noise of the marriage song, holding in my hand the hand of her that is dead; and after us followed a troop that magnified her and me, so noble a pair we were. And now with wailing instead of marriage songs, and garments of black for white wedding robes, I go to my desolate couch."

But while he yet lingered before the palace Hercules came back, leading with him a woman that was covered with a veil. And when he saw the King he said, " I hold it well to speak freely to one that is a friend, and that a man should not hide a grudge in his heart. Hear me, therefore. Though I was worthy to be counted thy friend, yet thou saidst not that thy wife lay dead in thy house, but suffered me to feast and make merry. For this, therefore, I blame thee. And now I will tell thee why I am returned. I pray thee, keep this woman against the day when I shall come back from the land of Thrace, bringing the horses of

King Diomed. And if it should fare ill with me, let her abide here and serve thee. Not without toil came she into my hands. I found as I went upon my way that certain men had ordered contests for wrestlers and runners, and the like. Now for them that had the preeminence in lesser things there were horses for prizes; and for the greater, as wrestling and boxing, a reward of oxen, to which was added this woman. And now I would have thee keep her, for which thing, haply, thou wilt one day thank me."

To this the King answered, "I thought no slight when I hid this truth from thee. Only it would have been for me sorrow upon sorrow if thou hadst gone to the house of another. But as for this woman, I would have thee ask this thing of some prince of Thessaly that hath not suffered such grief as I. In Pheræ here thou hast many friends; but I could not look upon her without tears. Add not then this new trouble. And also how could she, being young, abide in my house, for young I judge her to be? And of a truth, lady, thou art very like in shape and stature to my Alcestis that is dead. I pray you, take her from my sight, for she troubleth my heart, and my tears run over with beholding her."

Then said Hercules, "Would I had such strength that I could bring back thy wife from the dwellings of the dead, and put her in thy hands."

"I know thy good will, but what profiteth it? No man may bring back the dead."

"Well, time will soften thy grief, which yet is new."

"Yea, if by time thou meanest death."

"But a new wife will comfort thee."

"Hold thy peace; such a thing cometh not into my thoughts."

"What? wilt thou always keep this widowed state?"

"Never shall woman more be wife of mine."

"What will this profit her that is dead?"

"I know not, yet had I sooner die than be false to her."

"Yet I would have thee take this woman into thy house."

"Ask it not of me, I entreat thee, by thy father Zeus."

"Thou wilt lose much if thou wilt not do it."

"And if I do it I shall break my heart."

"Haply some day thou wilt thank me; only be persuaded."

"Be it so: they shall take the woman into the house."

"I would not have thee entrust her to thy servants."

"If thou so thinkest, lead her in thyself."

"Nay, but I would give her into thy hands."

"I touch her not, but my house she may enter."

"'Tis only to thy hand I entrust her."

"O King, thou compellest me to this against my will."

"Stretch forth thy hand and touch her."

"I touch her as I would touch the Gorgon's head."

"Hast thou hold of her?"

"I have hold."

"Then keep her safe, and say that the son of Zeus is a noble friend. See if she be like thy wife; and change thy sorrow for joy."

And when the King looked, lo! the veiled woman was Alcestis his wife.

THE STORY OF
THE VENGEANCE OF MEDEA.

JASON, being of right the prince of Iolcos in the land of Thessaly, came back to his kingdom. But Pelias, who had now for many years taken it for himself, spake him fair, and persuaded him that he should go on some adventure, and find glory and renown for himself, and so return; and he sware that afterwards he would peaceably give up the kingdom. Now in the land of Colchis, which lieth to the east of the sea which men call the Hospitable Sea, there was kept a great treasure, even the fleece of a great ram, which had been sacrificed there in time past. A marvellous beast was this ram, for it had flown through the air to Colchis from the land of Greece; and its fleece was of pure gold. So Jason gathered together many valiant men, sons of gods and heroes, such as were Hercules the son of Zeus, and Castor and Pollux, the twin brethren, and Calaïs and Zethus, that were sons to the North Wind, and Orpheus, that was the sweetest singer of all the dwellers upon earth. And they built for themselves a ship, and called its name the Argo, and so set sail, that they might bring back the fleece of gold to the land of Greece, to which, indeed, it rightfully belonged. Now when Jason and his fellows were come to Colchis, they asked the fleece of the king of the country. And he said that he would give it to them; only Jason must first yoke certain bulls that breathed fire from their nostrils, and slay a great dragon. But the Princess Medea saw Jason, and loved him, and purposed in her heart that she would help him. And being a great witch, and knowing all manner of drugs and enchantments, she gave him an ointment which kept all that anointed themselves with it so that they took no harm in battle with man or beast. But first Jason had promised, swearing to her a great oath, that she should be his wife, and that he would take her with him to the land of Greece, and that he would be faithful unto her to his life's end. So when he and his companions had yoked the bulls, and slain the dragon, and carried away the fleece, they took Medea with them in the ship, and so departed. But when Jason was come to the land of Iolcos, Pelias was not willing to keep his promise that he would give the kingdom to him. Whereupon Medea devised this thing against him. She took a ram, and cut him in pieces, and boiled his flesh in water, putting herbs into the caldron, and saying divers enchantments over it; and, lo! the beast came forth young, though it had been very old. Then she said to the daughters of Pelias, "Ye see this ram, how he was old, and I have made him young by boiling him in water. Do ye so likewise to your father, and I will help you with drugs and enchantments, as I did with the ram." But she lied unto them, and helped them not. So King Pelias died, being slain by his daughters, when they thought to make him young. But the people of the land were very wroth with Medea and with Jason her husband, and suffered them not to dwell there any more. So they came and dwelt in the land of Corinth. Now when they had abode there many days, the heart of Jason was turned away from his wife, and he was minded to put her away from him, and to take to himself another wife, even Glaucé, who was daughter to Creon, the King of the city.

Now, when this thing was told to Medea, at first she went through the house raging like a lioness that is bereaved of her whelps, and crying out to the Gods that they should smite the false husband that had sworn to her and had broken his oath, and affirming that she herself would take vengeance on him. And they that had the charge of her children kept them from her, lest she should do some mischief. But when her first fury was spent, she came forth from her house, and spake to certain women of Corinth of her acquaintance, that were gathered together to comfort her, and said, "I am come, my friends, to excuse myself to you. Ye know this sudden trouble that hath undone me, and the exceeding great wickedness of my husband. Surely we women are of all creatures that breathe the most miserable. For we must take husbands to rule over us, and how shall we know whether they be good or bad? Of a truth, a woman should have the gift of divination, that she may know what manner of man he is to whom she joineth herself, seeing that he is a stranger to her and unknown. If indeed she find one that is worthy, it is well with her; but if not, then had she better die. For a man, if he be troubled at home, goeth abroad, and holdeth converse with his friends and equals of age, and is comforted. But with a woman it is not so; for she hath only the life that is at home. But why do I compare myself with you? for ye dwell in your own land, and have parents and kinsfolk and friends; but I am desolate and without a country, and am wronged by this man that hath stolen me from a strange land; nor have I mother, or brother, or kinsman, who may help me in my need. This thing, therefore, I would ask of you; that if I can contrive any device by which I may have vengeance on my husband, and on him that giveth his daughter to him, and on the girl, ye keep silence. And vengeance I will have; for though a woman have not courage, nor dare to look upon the sword, yet if she be wronged in her love, there is nothing fiercer than she."

Then the women said, "We will keep silence as thou biddest us, for 'tis right that thou shouldest have vengeance on thy husband. But see! here cometh King Creon, doubtless with some new purpose."

And the King said, "Hear this, Medea. I bid thee depart out of this land, and thy children with thee. And I am come myself to execute this word, for I depart not again to my own house till I have cast thee forth from my borders."

Then Medea made answer, "Now am I altogether undone. But tell me, my lord, why dost thou drive me out of thy land?"

"Because I fear thee, lest thou should do some harm beyond all remedy to me and to my house. For I know that thou art wise, and hast knowledge of many curious arts; and besides, I hear that thou hast threatened grievous hurt against all that are concerned with this new marriage."

But Medea answered, "O my lord, this report of craft and wisdom hath wrought me harm not this day only, but many times! Truly it is not well that a man should teach

THE VENGEANCE OF MEDEA.   29

his children to be wise, for they gain thereby no profit, but hatred only. But as for me, my lord, my wisdom is but a small thing; nor is there cause why thou shouldest fear me. For who am I that I should transgress against a king? Nor indeed hast thou done me wrong. My husband, indeed, I hate; but thou hast given thy daughter as it pleased thee. The Gods grant that it may be well with thee and thine! Only suffer me to dwell in this land."

But the King would not, though she entreated him with many words. Only at the last he yielded this to her, that she might abide for one day and contrive some refuge for her children; "but," he said, "if thou tarry after this, thou and thy children, thou shalt surely die."

Then he went his way, and Medea said to the women that stood by, "That at least is well; be ye sure that there is evil to come for the bridegroom and the bride in this new marriage, and for their kin. Think ye that I had flattered this man but that I thought to gain somewhat thereby? Surely I had not touched his hand, no, nor spoken to him. And now—fool that he is—he hath given me this day, and when he might have driven me from the land he suffereth me to tarry. Verily he shall die for it, he and his daughter and this new bridegroom. But how shall I contrive it? Shall I put fire to the dwelling of the bride, or make my way by stealth into her chamber and slay her? Yet if I be found so doing, I shall perish, and my enemies will laugh me to scorn. Nay, let me work by poison, as is my wont. Well, and if they die, what then? What city will receive me? what friend shall give me protection? I know not. I will tarry awhile, and if some help appear, I will work my end with guile; but if not, I will take my sword and slay them that I hate, though I die. For by Hecaté, whom I reverence most of all the Gods, no man shall vex my heart and prosper. Therefore, Medea, fear not; use all thy counsel and craft. Shall the race of Sisyphus, shall Jason, laugh thee to scorn that art of the race of the Sun?"

When she had ended these words, there came Jason telling her that she did not well to be thus angry, and that she had brought upon herself this trouble of banishment by idle words against the rulers of the land; but that nevertheless he would have a care for her, and see that she wanted nothing needful. But when Medea heard him so speak, she burst out upon him in great fury, calling to mind how she had saved him once again from the bulls that breathed fire from their nostrils and from the great dragon that guarded the fleece of gold, and how she had done the old man Pelias to death for his sake; "and now," she said, "whither shall I go? who will receive me? for I have made enemies of my kinsfolk on account of thee, and now thou forsakest me. O Zeus! why can we discern false money from the true, but as for men, when we would know which is the good and which the bad, there is no mark by which we may know them?"

But to this Jason answered that if she had saved him in time past, she had done it of necessity, being compelled by love; and that he had made her a full recompense, taking her from a barbarous land to the land of Greece, where men lived by law and not by the will of the stronger and causing her to be highly reputed of for wisdom among the people of the land. "And as to this marriage," he said, "for which thou blamest me, I have made it in prudence and in care for thee and for thy children. For being an exile in this city, what could I do better than marry the daughter of the King? Nor is my heart turned from thee or from thy children. Only I have made provision against poverty, and that I might rear my sons in such fashion as befitted their birth. And now if thou needest aught in thy banishment, speak; for I would give thee provision without grudging, and also commend thee to such friends as I have."

"Keep thy gifts and thy friends," she said, "to thyself. There is no profit in that which cometh from such hands as thine."

So Jason went his way; and when he was departed there came Ægeus, King of Athens, who had been on a journey to inquire of the god at Delphi, for he was childless, and would fain have a son born to him. But he understood not what the god had answered, and was now on his way to King Pittheus of Trœzen, a man learned in such matters, that he might interpret the thing to him. And when he saw that Medea had been weeping, he would know

THE VENGEANCE OF MEDEA.

what ailed her. Then she told him how her husband was false to her, marrying a new wife, even the daughter of the king of the land, and how she was on the point to be banished, and her children with her. And when she saw that these things displeased King Ægeus, she said—

"Now, my lord, I beseech thee to have pity on me, nor suffer me to wander homeless and friendless, but receive me into thy house. So may the Gods grant thee thy desire that thou mayest have a son to reign after thee. And indeed I have such knowledge in these matters that I can help thee myself."

Then said King Ægeus, "I am willing to do thee this service both for right's sake and because of the hope of children which thou promisest to me. Only I may not take thee with me from this land. But if thou comest to me thou shalt be safe, nor will I give thee up to any man."

Then said Medea, "It is well, and I trust thee. And yet, for I am weak and my enemies are strong, I would fain bind thee by an oath."

To this the King answered, "Lady, thou art prudent, and I refuse not the oath; for being so bound, I shall have wherewith to answer thine enemies, if they seek thee from me. By what Gods shall I swear?"

"Swear by the Earth and by the Sun, who was the father of my father, and by all the Gods, that thou wilt not banish me from thy land, nor give me up to my enemies seeking me."

And King Ægeus sware a great oath, by the Earth and by the Sun, and by all the Gods, that he would not banish her, nor give her up; and so departed.

Then said Medea, "Now shall my counsels prosper; for this man hath given me that which I needed, even a refuge in the city of Athens. Now, therefore, hear what I will do. I will send one of my servants to Jason, and bid him come to me, and will speak softly to him, confessing that he hath done wisely in making this marriage with the daughter of King Creon. And I will ask of him that my children may remain in the land. And I will send them with a gift to this King's daughter, even a robe and a crown. But when she shall deck herself with them, she shall perish, so deadly are the poisons with which I shall anoint them. But very grievous is the deed that I must do when this shall have been accomplished. For after this I must slay my children. Nor shall any man deliver them out of my hand. Thus will I destroy the whole house of Jason, and so depart from the land. A very evil deed it is; but I cannot endure to be laughed to scorn by my enemies. And yet what profiteth me to live? For I have no country or home or refuge from trouble. I did evil leaving my father's house to follow this Greek. But verily he shall pay me to the very uttermost. For his children he shall see no more, and his bride shall perish miserably. Wherefore let no man henceforth think me to be weak or feeble."

And when the women would have turned her from her purpose, saying that so doing she would be the most miserable of women, she would not hearken, thinking only how she might best wound the heart of her husband.

Meanwhile a servant had carried the message to Jason. And when he was come, she said that she had repented of her anger against him, and that now he seemed to her to have done wisely, strengthening himself and his house by this marriage; and she prayed him that he would pardon her, being a woman and weak. And then she called to her children that they should come forth from the house, and take their father by his hand, for that her anger had ceased, and there was peace between them.

And Jason praised her that she had so changed her thoughts; and to his children he said, "Be sure, my sons, that your father hath counselled wisely for you. Live, you shall yet be the first in this land of Corinth."

And as he spake these words, he perceived that Medea wept, and said, "Why weepest thou?"

And she answered, "Women are always ready with tears for their children. I bare them; and when thou saidst to them 'Live,' I doubted whether this might be. But listen. Doubtless it is well that I depart from this land, both for me and for you. But as for these children, wilt thou not persuade the King that he suffer them to dwell here?"

"I know not whether I shall persuade him; but I will endeavour."

"Ask thy wife to intercede for these children, that they be not banished from this land."

"Even so. With her doubtless I shall prevail, if she be like to other women."

"I will help thee in this, sending her gifts so fair that there could be found nothing more beautiful on the earth—a robe exceeding fine and a crown of gold. These shall my children bear to her. So shall she be the happiest of women, having such a husband as thou art, and this adornment which the Sun, my grandsire, gave to his descendants after him that they should possess it."

Then she turned herself to her children, and said, "Take these caskets in your hands, my sons, and take them to the new bride, the King's daughter."

"But why wilt thou empty thy hands? Are there not, thinkest thou, robes enough and gold enough in the treasure of the King? Keep them for thyself. She will make more account of me than of thy gifts."

"Nay, not so. Is it not said that even the Gods are persuaded by gifts, and that gold is mightier than ten thousand speeches? Go, then, my children, to the King's palace. Seek your father's new wife, and fall down before her, and beseech her, giving her these adornments that ye be not banished from the land."

So the two boys went to the palace bearing the gifts. And all the servants of Jason that were therein rejoiced to see them, thinking that Medea had put away her anger against her husband. And they kissed their hands and their heads; and one led them into the chambers of the women, to the King's daughter. And she, who before sat looking with much love upon Jason, when she saw the boys, turned her head from them in anger.

But Jason soothed her, saying, "Be not angry with thy friends, but love them whom thy husband loveth, and take the gifts which they bring, and persuade thy father for my sake that he banish them not."

And when she saw the gifts, she changed her thoughts, and consented to his words. And in a very brief space she took the robe and clothed herself with it, and put the crown upon her head, and ordered her hair, looking in the glass and smiling at the image of herself. And then she rose from her seat, and walked through the house, stepping daintily, and often regarding herself.

But then befell a dreadful thing; for she grew pale, and trembled, and had well-nigh fallen upon the ground, scarce struggling to her chair.

And an old woman that was of her attendants set up a great cry, thinking that Pan or some other god had smitten her. But when she saw that she foamed at her mouth, and that her eyes rolled, and that there was no blood left in her, she ran to tell Jason of the matter, and another hastened to the King's chamber.

And then there came upon the maiden a greater woe than at the first, for there came forth a marvellous stream of fire from the crown of gold that was about her head, and all the while the robe devoured her flesh. Then she rose from her seat, and ran through the house, tossing her hair, and seeking to cast away the crown. But this she could not, for it clung to her very closely. And at the last she fell dead upon the ground, sorely disfigured so that none but her father only had known her. And all feared to touch her, lest they should be devoured also of the fire.

But when the King was come, he cast himself upon the dead body, saying, "O my child! what God hath so smitten thee? Why hast thou left me in my old age?"

And when he would have lifted himself, the robe held him fast, and he could not, though he struggled sorely. So he also died; and the two, father and daughter, lay together dead upon the ground.

Now in the meanwhile the old man that had the charge of the boys led them back to the house of the mother, and bade her rejoice, for that they were released from the sentence of banishment, and that some day she should also return by their means.

But the woman wept and answered doubtfully. Then she bade him go into the house and prepare for the lads what they might need for the day. And when he was departed she said, "O my sons, I go to a strange land and shall not see you come to fair estate and fortune; nor shall I make preparations for your marriage when you have grown to manhood. Vainly did

THE VENGEANCE OF MEDEA.

I bear you with pangs of travail; vainly did I rear you; vainly did I hope that ye should cherish me in my old age, and lay me out for my burial. O my children, why do ye so regard me? Why do ye laugh at me that shall never laugh again? Nay, I cannot do the deed. When I see the eyes of my children how bright they are, I cannot do it. And yet shall my enemies triumph over me and laugh me to scorn? Not so; I will dare it all." And she bade her children go into the house. But after a space she spake again, "O my heart, do not this deed. Spare my children! They will gladden thee in the land of thy banishment." And then again, after a space, "But no, it is otherwise ordained, and there is no escape. And I know that by this time the King's daughter hath the robe upon her and the crown about her head, and what I do I must do quickly."

Then she called to the boys again and said, "O my children! give me your right hands. O hands and mouths that I love, and faces fair exceedingly. Be ye happy—but not here. All that is here your father hath taken from you. O dear regard, O soft, soft flesh, O sweet, sweet breath of my children! Go, my children, go; I cannot look upon your faces any more."

And now there came a messenger from the King's palace and told her all that had there befallen. But when she heard it she knew that the time was come, and went into the house.

And the women that stood without heard a terrible cry from the children as they sought to flee from their mother and could not. And while they doubted whether they should not hasten within and, it might be, deliver them from their mother, came Jason to the gate and said to them, "Tell me, ladies, is Medea in this place, or hath she fled? Verily she must hide herself in the earth, or mount into the air, if she would not suffer due punishment for that which she hath done to the King and to his daughter. But of her I think not so much as of her children. For I would save them, lest the kinsmen of the dead do them some harm, seeking vengeance for the bloody deed of their mother."

Then the women answered, "O Jason, thou knowest not the truth, or thou wouldst not speak such words."

"How so? Would she kill me also?"

THE VENGEANCE OF MEDEA.

"Thy children are dead, slain by the hand of their mother."

"Dead are they? When did she slay them?"

"If thou wilt open the gates thou wilt see the dead corpses of thy children."

But when he battered at the gates, and cried out that they should open to him, he heard a voice from above, and saw Medea borne in a chariot, with winged dragons for horses, who cried to him, "Why seekest thou the dead and me that slew them? Trouble not thyself. If thou wantest aught of me, say on, but thou shalt never touch me with thy hand. For this chariot, which my father the Sun hath given me, shalt deliver me out of thy hands."

Then Jason cried, "Thou art an accursed woman, that hast slain thy own children with the sword, and yet darest to look upon the earth and the sun. What madness was it that I brought thee from thy own country to this land of Greece, for thou didst betray thy father and slay thy brother with the sword, and now thou hast killed thine own children, to avenge what thou deemest thine own wrong. No woman art thou, but a lioness or monster of the sea."

And to these things she answered, "Call me what thou wilt, lioness or monster of the sea; but this I know, that I have pierced thy heart. And as for thy children, thou shalt not touch them or see them any more; for I will bear them to the grove of Heré and bury them there, lest some enemy should break up their tomb and do them some dishonour. And I myself go to the land of Attica, where I shall dwell with King Ægeus, the son of Pandion. And as for thee, thou shalt perish miserably, for a beam from the ship Argo shall smite thee on the head. So shalt thou die.

Thus was the vengeance of Medea accomplished.

THE STORY OF THE DEATH OF HERCULES.

Œneus, who was king of the city of Pleuron in the land of Ætolia, had a fair daughter, Deïaneira by name. Now the maiden was sought in marriage by the god of the river Acheloüs; but she loved him not, for he was strange and terrible to look at. Sometimes he had the shape of a great dragon with scales, and sometimes he had the shape of a man, only that his head was the head of a bull, and streams of water flowed down from his beard. But it came to pass that Hercules, who was stronger than all the men that dwelt upon the earth, coming to the city of Pleuron, saw the maiden and loved her, and would have her to wife. And when she told him, saying that the river-god Acheloüs sought her in marriage, he bade her be of good courage, for that he would vanquish the creature in battle, so that it should not trouble her any more. Which thing he did, for when the river-god came, after his custom, Hercules did battle with him, and came nigh to strangling him, and brake off one of his horns. And the maiden looked on while the two fought together, and was well pleased that Hercules prevailed. King Œneus also was glad, and willingly gave her to him to wife. So after a while he departed with her unto his own country. And as they journeyed they came to the river Evenus. Now on the banks of this river there dwelt one Nessus, a centaur. (These centaurs had heads as the heads of men, but their bodies were like horses' bodies; and they were a savage race and a lawless.) This Nessus was wont to carry travellers across the river, which indeed was very broad and deep. And when he saw Deïaneira that she was very fair, he would have taken her from her husband; but Hercules drew his bow and smote him with an arrow.

Now when Nessus knew that he should die of his wound—for neither man nor beast lived

THE DEATH OF HERCULES.

that was wounded of these arrows—he thought in his wicked heart that he would be avenged on this man that had slain him. Whereupon he said to the woman, "Behold I die. But first I would give thee a gift. Take of the blood that cometh from this wound, and it shall come to pass that if the love of thy husband fail thee, thou shalt take of this blood and smear it on a garment, and give him the garment to wear, and he shall love thee again as at the first."

So the woman took of the blood and kept it by her. And it came to pass after a time that the two went to the city of Trachis and dwelt there. Now Trachis is in the land of Thessaly, near unto the springs of Œta. And Hercules loved his wife, and she dwelt in peace and happiness, only that he sojourned not long at home, but wandered over the face of the earth, doing many wonderful works at the commandment of Eurystheus, his brother. For the Gods had made Eurystheus to be master over him, for all that he was so strong. Now for the most part this troubled not his wife overmuch; for he departed from his house as one who counted it certain that he should return thereto.

But at the last this was not so. For he left a tablet wherein were written many things such as a man writeth who is about to die. For he had ordered therein the portion which his wife should have as her right of marriage, and how his possessions should be divided among his children. Also he wrote therein a certain space of time, even a year and three months, for when that was come to an end, he said, he must either be dead or have finished happily all his labours, and so be at peace continually. And this he had heard as an oracle from the doves that dwell in the oaks of Dodona. And when this time was well-nigh come to an end, Deïaneira, being in great fear, told the matter to Hyllus, her son. And even as she had ended, there came a messenger, saying, "Hail, lady! Put thy trouble from thee. The son of Alcmena lives and is well. This I heard from Lichas the herald; and hearing it I hastened to thee without delay, hoping that so I might please thee."

"But," said the Queen, "why cometh not the herald himself?"

"Because all the people stand about him, asking him questions, and hinder him."

THE DEATH OF HERCULES.

And not a long while after the herald came; and the name of the man was Lichas. And when the Queen saw him she cried, "What news hast thou of my husband? Is he yet alive?"

"Yea," said the herald, "he is alive and in good health."

"And where didst thou leave him? In some country of the Greeks, or among barbarians?"

"I left him in the land of Euboea, where he ordereth a sacrifice to Zeus."

"Payeth he thus some vow, or did some oracle command it?"

"He payeth a vow. And this vow he made before he took with his spear the city of these women whom thou seest."

"And who are these? For they are very piteous to behold."

"These he led captive when he destroyed the city of King Eurytus."

"And hath the taking of the city so long delayed him? For I have not seen him for the space of a year and three months."

"Not so. The most of this time he was a slave in the land of Lydia. For he was sold to Omphalé, who is Queen of that land, and served her. And how this came about I will tell thee. Thy husband sojourned in the house of King Eurytus, who had been long time his friend. But the King dealt ill with him, and spake to him unfriendly. For first he said that Hercules could not excel his sons in shooting with the bow, for all that he had arrows that missed not their aim. And next he reviled him, for that he was but a slave who served a free man, even King Eurystheus, his brother. And at the last, at a banquet, when Hercules was overcome with wine, the King cast him forth. Wherefore Hercules, being very wroth, slew the man. For the King came to the land of Tiryns, looking for certain horses, and Hercules caught him unawares, having his thoughts one way and his eyes another, and cast him down from the cliff that he died. Then Zeus was very wroth because he had slain him by craft, as he had never slain any man before, and caused that he should be sold for a year as a bond-slave to Queen Omphalé. And when the year was ended, and Hercules was free, he vowed a vow that he would destroy this city from which there had come to him this disgrace ; which vow he accomplished. And these women whom thou seest are the captives of his spear. And as for himself, be sure that thou wilt see him in no long space."

When Lichas had thus spoken, the Queen looked upon the captives, and had compassion on them, praying to the Gods that such an evil thing might not befall her children, or if, haply, it should befall them, she might be dead before. And seeing that there was one among them who surpassed the others in beauty, being tall and fair exceedingly, as if she were the daughter of a king, she would fain know who she was; and when the woman answered not a word, she would have the herald tell her. But he made as if he knew nothing at all; only that she seemed to be well born, and that from the first she had spoken nothing, but wept continually. And the Queen pitied her, and said that they should not trouble her, but take her into the palace and deal kindly with her, lest she should have sorrow upon sorrow.

But Lichas having departed for a space, the messenger that came at the first would have speech of the Queen alone. And when she had dismissed all the people, he told her that Lichas had not spoken truly, saying that he knew not who was this stranger, for that she was the daughter of King Eurytus, Iolé by name, and that indeed for love of her Hercules had taken the city.

And when the Queen heard this she was sore troubled, fearing lest the heart of her husband should now have been turned from her. But first she would know the certainty of the matter. So when Lichas came, being now about to depart, and inquired what he should say, as from the Queen to Hercules, she said to him, " Lichas, art thou one that loveth the truth ?"

" Yea, by Zeus !" said he, " if so be that I know it."

"Tell me, then, who is this woman whom thou hast brought?"

" A woman of Euboea ; but of what lineage I know not."

" Look thou here. Knowest thou who it is to whom thou speakest ?"

" Yea, I know it ; to Queen Deïaneira, daughter of Œneus and wife to Hercules, and my mistress."

THE DEATH OF HERCULES.

"Thou sayest that I am thy mistress. What should be done to thee if thou be found doing wrong to me?"

"What wrong? What meanest thou? But this is idle talk, and I had best depart."

"Thou departest not till I shall have inquired somewhat further of thee."

So the Queen commanded that they should bring the messenger who had set forth the whole matter to her. And when the man was come, and had told what he knew, and the Queen also spake fair, as bearing no wrath against her husband, Lichas made confession that the thing was indeed as the man had said, and that the woman was Iolé, daughter of King Eurytus.

Then the Queen took counsel with her companions, maidens that dwelt in the city of Trachis, and told them how she had a charm with her, the blood of Nessus the Centaur; and that Nessus had given it to her in old time because she was the last whom he carried over the river Evenus; and that it would win back for her the love of her husband. So she called Lichas, the herald, and said to him that he must do a certain thing for her. And he answered, "What is it, lady? Already I have lingered too long."

And she said, "Take now this robe, which thou seest to be fair and well woven, and carry it as a gift from me to my husband. And say to him from me that he suffer no man to wear it before him, and that the light of the sun touch it not, no, nor the light of a fire, till he himself shall clothe himself with it on a day on which he doeth sacrifice to the Gods. And say that I made this vow, if he should come back from this journey, that I would array him in this robe, wherein to do sacrifice. And that he may know thee to be a true messenger from me, take with thee this seal."

And Lichas said, "So surely as I know the craft of Hermes, who is the god of heralds, I will do this thing according to thy bidding."

Now the Queen had anointed the fair garment which she sent with the blood of Nessus the Centaur, that when her husband should clothe himself with it, his heart might be turned to her as at the first.

So Lichas the herald departed, bearing the

robe. But after no long time the Queen ran forth from the palace in great fear, wringing her hands, and crying to the maidens, her companions, that she was sore afraid lest in ignorance she had done some great mischief. And when they would know the cause of her grief and fear, she spake, saying, "A very marvellous and terrible thing hath befallen me. There was a morsel of sheep's wool which I dipped into the charm, even the blood of the Centaur, that I might anoint therewith the robe which ye saw me send to my husband. Now, this morsel of wool hath perished altogether. But that ye may understand this thing the better, I will set it forth to you at length. Know then that I have not forgotten aught of the things which the Centaur commanded me when he gave me this charm, but have kept them in my heart, even as if they were written on bronze. Now he bade me keep the thing where neither light of the sun nor fire might touch it. And this have I done; and when I anointed the robe, I anointed it in secret, in a certain dark place in the palace; but the morsel of wool wherewith I anointed it I threw, not heeding, into the sunshine. And, lo! it hath wasted till it is like unto dust which falleth when a man saweth wood. And from the earth whereon it lay there arise great bubbles of foam, like to the bubbles which arise when men pour into the vats the juice of the vine. And now I know not what I should say; for indeed, though I thought not so of the matter before, it seemeth not a thing to be believed that this Centaur should wish well to the man that slew him. Haply he deceived me, that he might work him woe. For I know that this is a very deadly poison, seeing that Chiron also suffered grievously by reason of it, albeit he was a god. Now if this be so, as I fear, then have I, and I only, slain my husband."

And she had scarce finished these words when Hyllus her son came in great haste; and when he saw her, he cried, "O my mother! would that I had found thee dead, or that thou wert not my mother, or that thou wert of a better mind than I know thee to be of."

But she said, "What have I done, my son, that thou so abhorrest me?"

"This day thou hast done my father to death."

THE DEATH OF HERCULES. 57

"What sayest thou? Who told thee this horrible thing that thou bringest against me?"

"I saw it with mine own eyes. And if thou wilt hear the whole matter, hearken. My father, having taken with his spear the city of Eurytus, went to a certain place hard by the sea, that he might offer sacrifices to Zeus, according to his vow. And even as he was about to begin, there came Lichas the herald bringing thy gift, the deadly robe. And he put it upon him as thou badest, and slew the beasts for the sacrifice, even twelve oxen chosen out of the prey, and one hundred other beasts. And for a while he did worship to the Gods with a glad heart, rejoicing in the beauty of his apparel. But when the fire grew hot, and the sweat came out upon his skin, the robe clung about him as though one had fitted it to him by art, and there went a great pang of pain through him, even as the sting of a serpent. And then he called to Lichas the herald, and would fain know for what end he had brought this accursed raiment. And when the wretch said that it was thy gift, he caught him by the foot, and cast him on a rock that was in the sea hard by, and all his brains were scattered upon it. And all the people groaned to see this thing, that the man perished so miserably, and that such madness wrought in thy husband. Nor did any one dare to draw near to him, for he threw himself now into the air, and now upon the ground, so fierce was the pain; and all the rocks about sounded again with his groaning. But after a while he spied me where I stood waiting in the crowd, and called to me, and said, 'Come hither, my son; fly not from me in my trouble, even if it needs be that thou die with me. But take me, and set me where no man may see me; but above all carry me from this land, that I die not here.' Whereupon we laid him in the hold of a ship, and brought him to this place, where thou wilt see him soon, either newly dead or on the point to die. This is what thou hast done, my mother; for thou hast slain thy husband, such a man as thou shalt never more see upon this earth."

And when the Queen heard this, she spake not a word, but hasted into the palace, and ran through it like unto one that is smitten with madness. And at the last she entered the

THE DEATH OF HERCULES.

chamber of Hercules, and sat down in the midst and wept piteously, saying, "O my marriage-bed, where never more I shall lie, farewell!" And as she spake she loosed the golden brooch that was upon her heart, and bared all her left side; and before any could hinder her—for her nurse had seen what she did, and had run to fetch her son—she took a two-edged sword and smote herself to the heart, and so fell dead. And as she fell there came her son, that now knew from them of the household how she had been deceived of that evil beast the Centaur, and fell upon her with many tears and cries, saying that now he was bereaved both of father and of mother in one day.

But while he lamented, there came men bearing Hercules in a litter. He was asleep, for the pain had left him for a space, and the old man that was guide to the company was earnest with Hyllus that he should not wake his father. Nevertheless, Hercules heard the young man's voice, and his sleep left him. Then he cried aloud in his agony, complaining to Zeus that he had suffered such a torment to come upon him, and reproaching them that stood by that they gave him not a sword wherewith he might make an end to his pain. But most of all he cursed his wife that she had wrought him such woe, saying to Hyllus—

"See now, my son, how that this treacherous woman hath worked such pain to me as I have never endured before in all the earth, through which, as thou knowest, I have journeyed, cleansing it from all manner of monsters. And now thou seest how I, who have subdued all things, weep and cry as doth a girl. And these hands and arms, with which I slew the lion that wasted the land of Nemea and the great dragon of Lerna, and dragged into the light the three-headed dog that guardeth the gate of hell, see how these, which no man yet hath vanquished in fight, are wasted and consumed with the fire. But there is one thing which they shall yet do, for I will slay her that wrought this deed."

Then Hyllus made answer, "My father, suffer me to speak, for I have that to tell thee of my mother which thou shouldest hear."

"Speak on; but beware that thou show not thyself vile, excusing her."

"She is dead."

"Who slew her? This is a strange thing thou tellest."

"She slew herself with her own hand."

"'Tis ill done. Would that I had slain her myself!"

"Thy heart will be changed towards her when thou hearest all."

"This is strange indeed; but say on."

"All that she did she did with good intent."

"With good intent, thou wicked boy, when she slew her husband?"

"She sought to keep thy love, fearing that thy heart was turned to another."

"And who of the men of Trachis is so cunning in leechcraft?"

"The Centaur Nessus gave her the poison long since, saying that she might thus win back thy love."

And when Hercules heard this he cried aloud, "Then is my doom come; for long since it was prophesied to me that I should not die by the hand of any living creature, but by one that dwelt in the region of the dead. And now this Centaur, whom I slew long ago, hath slain me in turn. And now, my son, hearken unto me. Thou knowest the hill of Œta. Carry me thither thyself, taking also such of thy friends as thou wilt have with thee. And build there a great pile of oak and wild olive, and lay me thereon, and set fire thereto. And take heed that thou shed no tear nor utter a cry, but work this deed in silence, if, indeed, thou art my true son: and if thou doest not so, my curse shall be upon thee for ever."

And Hyllus vowed that he would do this thing, only that he could not set fire to the pile with his own hand. So they bare Hercules to the top of the hill of Œta, and built a great pile of wood, and laid him thereon. And Philoctetes, who was of the companions of Hyllus, set fire to the pile. For which deed Hercules gave to him his bow and the arrows that missed not their aim. And the tale of this bow, and how it fared with him that had it, may be read in the story of Philoctetes.

THE STORY OF THE
SEVEN CHIEFS AGAINST THEBES.

It befell in times past that the Gods, being angry with the inhabitants of Thebes, sent into their land a very noisome beast which men called the Sphinx. Now this beast had the face and breast of a very fair woman, but the feet and claws of a lion; and it was wont to ask a riddle of such as encountered it; and such as answered not aright it would tear and devour. Now when it had laid waste the land many days, there chanced to come to Thebes one Œdipus, who had fled from the city of Corinth that he might escape the doom which the Gods had spoken against him. And the men of the place told him of the Sphinx, how she cruelly devoured the people, and that he who should deliver them from her should have the kingdom. So Œdipus, being very bold, and also ready of wit, went forth to meet the monster. And when she saw him she spake, saying—

> "Read me this riddle right, or die :
> What liveth there beneath the sky,
> Four-footed creature that doth choose
> Now three feet and now twain to use,
> And still more feebly o'er the plain
> Walketh with three feet than with twain?"

And Œdipus made reply—

> "'Tis man, who in life's early day
> Four-footed crawleth on his way ;
> When time hath made his strength complete,
> Upright his form and twain his feet ;
> When age hath bowed him to the ground
> A third foot in his staff is found."

And when the Sphinx found that her riddle was answered, she cast herself from a high rock and perished. Now for a while Œdipus reigned in great power and glory ; but afterwards his doom came upon him, so that in his madness he put out his own eyes. Then his two sons cast him into prison, and took his kingdom, making agreement between themselves that each should reign for the space of one year. And the elder of the two, whose name was Eteocles, first had the kingdom ; but when his year was come to an end, he would not abide by his promise, but kept that which he should have given up, and drave out his younger brother from the city. Then the younger, whose name was Polynices, fled to Argos, to King Adrastus. And after a while he married the daughter of the King, who made a covenant with him that he would bring him back with a high hand to Thebes, and set him on the throne of his father. Then the King sent messengers to certain of the princes of Greece, entreating that they would help in this matter. And of these some would not, but others hearkened to his words, so that a great army was gathered together and followed the King and Polynices to make war against Thebes. So they came and pitched their camp over against the city. And after that they had fought against it many days, and yet had prevailed nothing, Adrastus held a council of the chiefs, and it was agreed that next day, early in the morning, they should assault the city with all their might. And when the morning was come, the chiefs were gathered together, being seven in number. And first of all they slew a bull, and caught the blood of the beast in the hollow of a shield, into which they dipped their hands, and sware a great oath that they would take the city of Thebes or die. And having sworn, they hung upon the chariot of Adrastus what should be memorials of them each for his own father and mother, all weeping the while. After this they cast lots for the places which they should take, for there were seven gates to the city, that each chief might assault a gate.

But their purpose was known to the King Eteocles, for he had heard the whole matter from Tiresias, the wise seer, who told beforehand all that should come to pass, discovering it from the voice of birds, for being blind he could not judge from their flight, or from the tokens of fire, as other soothsayers are wont. Wherefore the King gathered together all that could bear arms, even youths not grown, and old men that were waxed feeble with age, and bade them fight for the land, for "she," he said, "gave you birth and reared you, and now asketh that ye help her in this her need. And though hitherto we have fared well in this war, know ye for certain, for Tiresias the soothsayer hath said it, that there cometh a great danger this day upon the city. Wherefore haste ye to the battlements, and to the towers that are upon the walls, and take your stand in the gates, and be of good courage, and quit you like men."

And as he made an end of speaking there ran in one who declared that even now the enemy was about to assault the city. And after him came a troop of maidens of Thebes, crying out that the enemy had come forth from the camp, and that they heard the tramp of many feet upon the earth, and the rattling of shields, and the noise of many spears. And they lifted up their voices to the Gods that they should help the city, to Ares, the god of the golden helmet, that he should defend the land which in truth was his from old time, and to Father Zeus, and to Pallas, who was the daughter of Zeus, and to Poseidon, the great ruler of the sea, and to Aphrodité the Fair, for that she was the mother of their race, and to Apollo, the wolf-king, that he would be as a devouring wolf to the enemy, and to Artemis, that she should bend her bow against them, and to Heré, the Queen of heaven, even to all the dwellers in Olympus, that they should defend the city, and save it.

But the King was very wroth when he heard this outcry, and cried, "Think ye to make bold the hearts of our men by these lamentations? Now may the Gods save me from this race of women; for if they be bold no man can endure their insolence, and if they be afraid they vex both their home and their country. Even so now do ye help them that are without and trouble your own people. But hearken to this. He that heareth not my command, be he man or woman, the people shall stone him. Speak I plainly?"

"But, O son of Œdipus," the maidens made reply, "we hear the rolling of the chariot wheels, and the rattling of the axles, and the jingling of the bridle reins."

"What then?" said the King, "if the ship labour in the sea, and the helmsman leave the helm and fly to the prow that he may pray before the image, doeth he well?"

"Nay, blame us not that we came to beseech the Gods when we heard the hailstorm of war rattling on the gates."

SEVEN CHIEFS AGAINST THEBES.

" 'Tis well," cried the King, " yet men say that the Gods leave the city that is at the point to fall. And mark ye this, that safety is the child of obedience. But as for duty, 'tis for men to do sacrifice to the Gods, and for women to keep silence and to abide at home."

But the maidens made reply, " 'Tis the Gods who keep this city, nor do they transgress who reverence them."

" Yes, but let them reverence them in due order. And now hearken to me. Keep ye silence. And when I have made my prayer, raise ye a joyful shout that shall gladden the hearts of our friends and put away all fear from them. And to the Gods that keep this city I vow that if they give us victory in this war I will sacrifice to them sheep and oxen, and will hang up in their houses the spoils of the enemy. And now, ye maidens, do ye also make your prayers, but not with vain clamour. And I will choose seven men, being myself the seventh, who shall meet the seven that come against the gates of our city."

Then the King departed, and the maidens made their prayer after this fashion: " My heart feareth as a dove feareth the serpent for her young ones, so cruelly doth the enemy come about this city to destroy it! Shall ye find elsewhere as fair a land, ye Gods, if ye suffer this to be laid waste, or streams as sweet? Help us then, for indeed it is a grievous thing when men take a city, for the women, old and young, are dragged by the hair, and the men are slain with the sword, and there is slaughter and burning, while they that plunder cry each man to his comrade, and the fruits of the earth are wasted upon the ground; nor is there any hope but in death."

And as they made an end, the King came back, and at the same time a messenger bringing tidings of the battle, how the seven chiefs had ranged themselves each against a gate of the city. And the man's story was this.

"First Tydeus, the Ætolian, standeth in great fury at the gate of Prœtus. Very wroth is he because the soothsayer, Amphiaraüs, suffereth him not to cross the Ismenus, for that the omens promise not victory. A triple crest he hath, and there are bells of bronze under his shield which ring terribly. And on his shield he hath this device: the heaven studded with stars, and in the midst the mightiest of the stars, the eye of night, even the moon. Whom, O King, will thou set against this man?"

Then the King made reply, "I tremble not at any man's adorning, and a device woundeth not. And, indeed, as for the night that thou tellest to be on his shield, haply it signifieth the night of death that shall fall upon his eyes. Over against him will I set the son of Astacus, a brave man and a modest. Also he is of the race of the Dragon's Teeth, and men call him Melanippus."

And the messenger said, "Heaven send him good fortune! At the gate of Electra standeth Capaneus, a man of great stature, and his boastings are above all measure, for he crieth out that he will destroy this city whether the Gods will or no, and that Zeus with his thunder shall not stay him, for that the thunder is but as the sun at noon. And on his shield he hath a man bearing a torch, and these words, 'I WILL BURN THIS CITY.' Who now shall stand against this boaster and fear not?"

Then the King said, "His boastings I heed

not. They shall turn to his own destruction. For as he sendeth out swelling words against Zeus, so shall Zeus send against him the thunder, smiting him, but not of a truth as the sun smiteth. Him shall Polyphantus encounter, a valiant man and dear to Queen Artemis."

"He that is set against the gate of Neïs is called Eteoclus by name. He driveth a chariot with four horses, in whose nostrils are pipes making a whistling noise, after the fashion of barbarians. And on his shield he hath this device: a man mounting a ladder that is set against a tower upon a wall, and with it these words, 'NOT ARES' SELF SHALL DRIVE ME HENCE.' See that thou set a fit warrior against him."

"Megareus, son of Creon, of the race of the Dragon, shall fight against him, who will not leave the gate for any whistling noise of horses; for either he will die as a brave man dieth for his country, or will take a double spoil, even this boaster and him also that he beareth upon his shield."

"At the next gate to this, even the gate of Athené, standeth Hippomedon. A great shield and a terrible he hath, and on it this device, which no mean workman hath wrought: Typhon breathing out a great blast of black smoke, and all about it serpents twined together. And the man also is terrible as his shield, and seemeth to be inspired of Ares. Whom wilt thou set against this man, O King?"

"First shall Pallas stand against him and drive him from this city, even as a bird driveth a snake from her young ones. And next I have set Hyperbius, son of Œneus, to encounter him, being inferior neither in form nor courage, nor yet in skill of arms, and also dear to Hermes. Enemies shall they be, bearing also on their shields gods that are enemies, for Hippomedon hath Typhon, but Hyperbius hath Zeus; and even as Zeus prevailed over Typhon, so also shall Hyperbius prevail over this man."

"So be it, O King. Know also that at the north gate is set Parthenopæus the Arcadian. Very young is he, and fair also to behold, and his mother was the huntress Atalanta. This man sweareth by his spear, which he holdeth to be better than all gods whatsoever, that he will lay waste this city. And on his shield he beareth a device, the Sphinx, which holdeth in her claws one of the sons of Cadmus."

"Against this Arcadian will I set Actor, brother to Hyperbius, no boaster but a man of deeds, who will not let this hateful monster, the Sphinx, pass thus into the city; but will rather make it ill content to have come hither, so many and fierce blows shall he deal it."

"Hear now of the sixth among the chiefs, the wise soothsayer, Amphiaraüs. Ill pleased is he with these things, for against Tydeus he uttereth many reproaches, that he is an evil counsellor to Argos and to King Adrastus, stirring up strife and slaughter. And to thy brother also he speaketh in like fashion, saying, 'Is this a thing that the Gods love, and that men shall praise in the days to come, that thou bringest a host of strangers to lay waste the city of thy fathers? Shall this land, if thou subduest it by the spear of the enemy, ever make alliance with thee? As for me I shall fall in this land, for am I not a seer? Be it so. I shall not die without honour!' No device hath this man on his shield, for he seeketh not to seem, but to be in very deed most excellent.

Thou must need send some wise man to stand against him."

"It is an ill fate that bringeth a just man into company with the wicked. And of a truth there is not a worse thing upon the earth than ill companionship, wherein the sowing is madness and the harvest is death. For thus a god-fearing man being on shipboard with godless companions perisheth with them; and one that is righteous, if he dwell in one city with the wicked, is destroyed with the same destruction. So shall it fare with this Amphiaraüs; for though he be a good man and righteous, and that feareth God, yet shall he perish because he beareth these boasters company. And I think that he will not come near to the gates, so well knoweth he what shall befall him. Yet have I set Lasthenes to stand against him, young in years but old in counsel, very keen of eye, and swift of hand to cast his javelin from under his shield."

"And now, O King! hear how thy brother beareth himself, for he it is who standeth yonder at the seventh gate. For he crieth aloud that he will climb upon the wall and slay thee, even though he die with thee, or drive thee forth into banishment, even as thou, he saith, hast driven him. And on his shield there is this device: a woman leading an armed man, and while she leadeth him, she saith, 'I AM JUSTICE, AND I WILL BRING BACK THIS MAN TO THE KINGDOM WHICH IS HIS OF RIGHT.'"

But when the King heard this he brake forth in much fury, "Now will the curse of this house be fulfilled to the uttermost. Yet must I not bewail myself, lest there should fall upon us an evil that is yet greater than this. And as for this Polynices, thinketh he that signs and devices will give him that which he coveteth? Thinketh he that Justice is on his side? Nay, but from the day that he came forth from the womb he hath had no converse with her, neither will she stand by him this day. I will fight against him. Who more fit than I? Bring forth my armour that I may make ready."

And though the maidens entreated with many words that he would not do this thing, but leave the place to some other of the chiefs, saying that there was no healing or remedy for a brother's blood shed in such fashion, he would not hearken, but armed himself and went forth to the battle. Thus ever doth the madness of men work out to the full the curses of the Gods.

Then the battle grew fierce about the wall, and the men of Thebes prevailed. For when Parthenopæus, the Arcadian, fell like a whirlwind upon the gate that was over against him, Actor the Theban smote him on the head with a great stone, and brake his head, so that he fell dead upon the ground. And when Capaneus assaulted the city, crying that not even the Gods should stay him, there came upon him the wrath which he defied; for when he had mounted the ladder and was now about to leap upon the battlements, Zeus smote him with the thunderbolt, and there was no life left in him, so fierce was the burning heat of the lightning. But the chiefest fight was between the two brothers; and this, indeed, the two armies stood apart to see. For the two came together in an open space before the gates; and first Polynices prayed to Heré, for she was the goddess of the great city of Argos, which had helped him in this enterprise, and Eteocles prayed to Pallas of the Golden Shield, whose temple stood hard by. Then they crouched, each covered with his shield, and holding his spear in his hand, if by chance his enemy should give occasion to smite him; and if one showed so much as an eye above the rim of his shield the other would strike at him. But after a while King Eteocles slipped upon a stone that was under his foot, and uncovered his leg, at which straightway Polynices took aim with his spear, piercing the skin. And the men of Argos shouted to see it. But so doing he laid his own shoulder bare, and King Eteocles gave him a wound in the breast; and then the men of Thebes shouted for joy. But he brake his spear in striking, and would have fared ill but that with a great stone he smote the spear of Polynices, and brake this also in the middle. And now were the two equal, for each had lost his spear. So they drew their swords and came yet closer together. But Eteocles used a device which he had learnt in the land of Thessaly; for he drew his left foot back, as if he would have ceased from the battle, and then of a sudden moved the right forward; and so smiting sideways, drave his sword right through the body of Polynices. But when thinking that he had slain him he set his weapons in the earth, and began to spoil him of his arms, the other, for he yet breathed a little, laid his hand upon his sword, and though he had scarce strength to smite, yet gave the King a mortal blow, so that the two lay dead together on the plain. And the men of Thebes lifted up the bodies of the dead, and bare them both into the city.

So was the doom of the house of Œdipus accomplished ; and yet not all, as shall be told in the story of Antigone, who was the sister of these two.

THE STORY OF ANTIGONE.

When the two brothers, the sons of King Œdipus, had fallen each by the hand of the other, the kingdom fell to Creon their uncle. For not only was he the next of kin to the dead, but also the people held him in great honour because his son Menœceus had offered himself with a willing heart that he might deliver his city from captivity. Now when Creon was come to the throne, he made a proclamation about the two Princes, commanding that they should bury Eteocles with all honour, seeing that he died as beseemed a good man and a brave, doing battle for his country, that it should not be delivered into the hands of the enemy; but as for Polynices he bade them leave his body to be devoured by the fowls of the air and the beasts of the field, because he had joined himself to the enemy, and would have beaten down the walls of the city, and burned the temples of the Gods with fire, and led the people captive. Also he commanded that if any man should break this decree he should suffer death by stoning.

Now Antigone, who was sister to the two Princes, heard that the decree had gone forth, and chancing to meet her sister Ismené before the gates of the palace, spake to her, saying, "O my sister, hast thou heard this decree that the King hath put forth concerning our brethren that are dead?"

Then Ismené made answer, "I have heard nothing, my sister, only that we are bereaved of both of our brethren in one day, and that the army of the Argives is departed in this night that is now past. So much I know, but no more."

"Hearken then. King Creon hath made a proclamation that they shall bury Eteocles with all honour; but that Polynices shall lie unburied, that the birds of the air and the beasts of the field may devour him; and that whosoever shall break this decree shall suffer death by stoning."

"But if it be so, my sister, how can we avail to change it?"

"Think whether or no thou wilt share with me the doing of this deed."

"What deed? What meanest thou?"

"To pay due honour to this dead corpse."

"What? Wilt thou bury him when the King hath forbidden it?"

"Yea, for he is my brother and also thine, though, perchance, thou wouldst not have it so. And I will not play him false."

"O my sister, wilt thou do this when Creon hath forbidden it?"

"Why should he stand between me and mine?"

"But think now what sorrows are come upon our house. For our father perished miserably, having first put out his own eyes; and our mother hanged herself with her own hands; and our two brothers fell in one day, each by the other's spear; and now we two only are left. And shall we not fall into a worse destruction than any, if we transgress these commands of the King? Think, too, that we are women and not men, and must of necessity obey them that are stronger. Wherefore, as for me, I will pray the dead to pardon me, seeing that I am thus constrained; but I will obey them that rule."

"I advise thee not, and, if thou thinkest thus, I would not have thee for helper. But know that I will bury my brother, nor could I better die than for doing such a deed. For as he loved me, so also do I love him greatly. And shall not I do pleasure to the dead rather than to the living, seeing that I shall abide with the dead for ever? But thou, if thou wilt, do dishonour to the laws of the Gods."

"I dishonour them not. Only I cannot set myself against the powers that be."

"So be it: but I will bury my brother."

"O my sister, how I fear for thee!"

"Fear for thyself. Thine own lot needeth all thy care."

"Thou wilt at least keep thy counsel, nor tell the thing to any man."

"Not so: hide it not. I shall scorn thee more if thou proclaim it not aloud to all."

So Antigone departed; and after a while came to the same place King Creon, clad in his royal robes, and with his sceptre in his hand, and set forth his counsel to the elders who were assembled, how he had dealt with the two Princes according to their deserving, giving all honour to him that loved his country, and casting forth the other unburied. And he bade them take care that this decree should be kept, saying that he had also appointed certain men to watch the dead body.

But he had scarcely left speaking, when there came one of these same watchers and said, "I have not come hither in haste, O King, nay, I doubted much, while I was yet on the way, whether I should not turn again. For now I thought, 'Fool, why goest thou where thou shalt suffer for it;' and then again, 'Fool, the King will hear the matter elsewhere, and then how wilt thou fare?' But at the last I came as I had purposed, for I know that nothing may happen to me contrary to fate."

"But say," said the King, "what troubles thee so much?"

"First hear my case. I did not the thing, and know not who did it, and it were a grievous wrong should I fall into trouble for such a cause."

"Thou makest a long preface, excusing thyself, but yet hast, as I judge, something to tell."

THE STORY OF ANTIGONE. 85

"Fear, my lord, ever causeth delay."

"Wilt thou not speak out thy news and then begone?"

"I will speak it. Know then that some man hath thrown dust upon this dead corpse, and done besides such things as are needful."

"What sayest thou? Who hath dared to do this deed?"

"That I know not, for there was no mark as of spade or pick-axe; nor was the earth broken, nor had waggon passed thereon. We were sore dismayed when the watchman showed the thing to us; for the body we could not see. Buried indeed it was not, but rather covered with dust. Nor was there any sign as of wild beast or of dog that had torn it. Then there arose a contention among us, each blaming the other, and accusing his fellows, and himself denying that he had done the deed or was privy to it. And doubtless we had fallen to blows but that one spake a word which made us all tremble for fear, knowing that it must be as he said. For he said that the thing must be told to thee, and in no wise hidden. So we drew lots, and by evil chance the lot fell upon me. Wherefore I am here, not willingly, for no man loveth him that bringeth ill tidings."

Then said the chief of the old men, "Consider, O King, for haply this thing is from the Gods."

But the King cried, "Thinkest thou that the Gods care for such an one as this dead man, who would have burnt their temples with fire, and laid waste the land which they love, and set at naught the laws? Not so. But there are men in this city who have long time had ill will to me, not bowing their necks to my yoke; and they have persuaded these fellows with money to do this thing. Surely there never was so evil a thing as money, which maketh cities into ruinous heaps, and banisheth men from their houses, and turneth their thoughts from good unto evil. But as for them that have done this deed for hire, of a truth they shall not escape, for I say to thee, fellow, if ye bring not here before my eyes the man that did this thing, I will hang you up alive. So shall ye learn that ill gains bring no profit to a man."

So the guard departed; but as he went he said to himself, "Now may the Gods grant that the man be found; but however this may be, thou shalt not see me come again on such errand as this, for even now have I escaped beyond all hope." Notwithstanding, after a space he came back with one of his fellows; and they brought with them the maiden Antigone, with her hands bound together. And it chanced that at the same time King Creon came forth from the palace. Then the guard set forth the thing to him, saying, "We cleared away the dust from the dead body, and sat watching it. And when it was now noon, and the sun was at his height, there came a whirlwind over the plain, driving a great cloud of dust. And when this had passed, we looked, and lo! this maiden whom we have brought hither stood by the dead corpse. And when she saw that it lay bare as before, she sent up an exceeding bitter cry, even as a bird whose young ones have been taken from the nest. Then she cursed them that had done this deed; and brought dust and sprinkled it upon the dead man, and poured water upon him three times. Then we ran and laid hold upon her, and accused her that she had done this deed; and she denied it not. But as for me, 'tis well to have escaped from death, but it is ill to bring friends into the same. Yet I hold that there is nothing dearer to a man than his life."

Then said the King to Antigone, "Tell me in a word, didst thou know my decree?"

"I knew it. Was it not plainly declared?"

"How daredst thou to transgress the laws?"

"Zeus made not such laws, nor Justice that dwelleth with the Gods below. I judged not that thy decrees had such authority that a man should transgress for them the unwritten sure commandments of the Gods. For these, indeed, are not of to-day or yesterday, but they live for ever, and their beginning no man knoweth. Should I, for fear of thee, be found guilty against them? That I should die I knew. Why not? All men must die. And if I die before my time, what loss? He who liveth among many sorrows, even as I have lived, counteth it gain to die. But had I left my own mother's son unburied, this had been loss indeed."

Then said the King, "Such stubborn thoughts have a speedy fall, and are shivered even as the iron that hath been made hard in the furnace. And as for this woman and her sister—for I judge her sister to have had a part in this matter

—though they were nearer to me than all my kindred, yet shall they not escape the doom of death. Wherefore let some one bring the other woman hither."

And while they went to fetch the maiden Ismené, Antigone said to the King, "Is it not enough for thee to slay me? What need to say more? For thy words please me not nor mine thee. Yet what nobler thing could I have done than to bury my own mother's son? And so would all men say but fear shutteth their mouths."

"Nay," said the King, "none of the children of Cadmus thinketh thus, but thou only. But, hold, was not he that fell in battle with this man thy brother also?"

"Yes, truly, my brother he was."

"And dost thou not dishonour him when thou honourest his enemy?"

"The dead man would not say it, could he speak."

"Shall then the wicked have like honour with the good?"

"How knowest thou but that such honour pleaseth the Gods below?"

"I have no love for them I hate, though they be dead."

"Of hating I know nothing; 'tis enough for me to love."

"If thou wilt love, go love the dead. But while I live no woman shall rule me."

Then those that had been sent to fetch the maiden Ismené brought her forth from the palace. And when the King accused her that she had been privy to the deed she denied not, but would have shared one lot with her sister. But Antigone turned from her, saying, "Not so; thou hast no part or lot in the matter. For thou hast chosen life, and I have chosen death; and even so shall it be." And when Ismené saw that she prevailed nothing with her sister, she turned to the King and said, "Wilt thou slay the bride of thy son?"

"Aye," said he, "there are other brides to win!"

"But none," she made reply, "that accord so well with him."

"I will have no evil wives for my sons," said the King.

Then cried Antigone, "O Hæmon, whom I love, how thy father wrongeth thee!"

Then the King bade the guards lead the two into the palace. But scarcely had they gone when there came to the place the Prince Hæmon, the King's son, who was betrothed to the maiden Antigone. And when the King saw him, he said, "Art thou content, my son, with thy father's judgment?"

And the young man answered, "My father, I would follow thy counsels in all things."

Then said the King, "'Tis well spoken, my son. This is a thing to be desired, that a man should have obedient children. But if it be otherwise with a man, he hath gotten great trouble for himself, and maketh sport for them that hate him. And now as to this matter. There is nought worse than an evil wife. Wherefore I say, let this damsel wed a bridegroom among the dead. For since I have found her, alone of all this people, breaking my decree, surely she shall die. Nor shall it profit her to claim kinship with me, for he that would rule a city must first deal justly with his own kindred. And as for obedience, this it is that maketh a city to stand both in peace and in war."

To this the Prince Hæmon made answer,

"What thou sayest, my father, I do not judge. Yet bethink thee, that I see and hear on thy behalf what is hidden from thee. For common men cannot abide thy look if they say that which pleaseth thee not. Yet do I hear it in secret. Know then that all the city mourneth for this maiden, saying that she dieth wrongfully for a very noble deed, in that she buried her brother. And 'tis well, my father, not to be wholly set on thy own thoughts, but to listen to the counsels of others."

"Nay," said the King; "shall I be taught by such an one as thou?"

"I pray thee regard my words, if they be well, and not my years."

"Can it be well to honour them that transgress? And hath not this woman transgressed?"

"The people of this city judgeth not so."

"The people, sayest thou? Is it for them to rule, or for me?"

"No city is the possession of one man only."

So the two answered one the other, and their anger waxed hot. And at the last the King cried, "Bring this accursed woman, and slay her before his eyes."

And the Prince answered, "That thou shalt never do. And know this also, that thou shalt never see my face again."

So he went away in a rage; and the old men would have appeased the King's wrath, but he would not hearken to them, but said that the two maidens should die. "Wilt thou then slay them both?" said the old men.

"'Tis well said," the King made answer. "Her that meddled not with the matter I harm not."

"And how wilt thou deal with the other?"

"There is a desolate place, and there I will shut her up alive in a sepulchre; yet giving her so much of food as shall quit us of guilt in the matter, for I would not have the city defiled. There let her persuade Death, whom she loveth so much, that he harm her not."

So the guards led Antigone away to shut her up alive in the sepulchre. But scarcely had they departed when there came the old prophet Tiresias, seeking the King. Blind he was, so that a boy led him by the hand; but the Gods had given him to see things to come. And when the King saw him he asked, "What seekest thou, wisest of men?"

Then the prophet answered, "Hearken, O King, and I will tell thee. I sat in my seat, after my custom, in the place whither all manner of birds resort. And as I sat I heard a cry of birds that I knew not, very strange and full of wrath. And I knew that they tare and slew each other, for I heard the fierce flapping of their wings. And being afraid, I made inquiry about the fire, how it burned upon the altars. And this boy, for as I am a guide to others so he guideth me, told me that it shone not at all, but smouldered and was dull, and that the flesh which was burnt upon the altar spluttered in the flame, and wasted away into corruption and filthiness. And now I tell thee, O King, that the city is troubled by thy ill counsels. For the dogs and the birds of the air tear the flesh of this dead son of Œdipus, whom thou sufferest not to have due burial, and carry it to the altars, polluting them therewith. Wherefore the Gods receive not from us prayer or sacrifice; and the cry of the birds hath an evil sound, for they are full of the flesh of a man. Therefore I bid the be wise in time. For all men may err; but he that keepeth not his folly, but repenteth, doeth well; but stubbornness cometh to great trouble."

Then the King answered, "Old man, I know the race of prophets full well, how ye sell your art for gold. But, make thy trade as thou wilt, this man shall not have burial; yea, though the eagles of Zeus carry his flesh to their master's throne in heaven, he shall not have it."

And when the prophet spake again, entreating him, and warning, the King answered him after the same fashion, that he spake not honestly, but had sold his art for money. But at the last the prophet spake in great wrath, saying, "Know, O King, that before many days shall pass, thou shalt pay a life for a life, even one of thine own children, for them with whom thou hast dealt unrighteously, shutting up the living with the dead, and keeping the dead from them to whom they belong. Therefore the Furies lie in wait for thee, and thou shalt see whether or no I speak these things for money. For there shall be mourning and lamentation in thine own house; and against thy people shall be stirred up all the cities, whose sons thou hast made to lie unburied. And now, my child, lead me home, and let this man rage against them that are younger than I."

So the prophet departed, and the old men were sore afraid, and said, " He hath spoken terrible things, O King; nor ever since these gray hairs were black have we known him say that which was false."

" Even so," said the King," and I am troubled in heart, and yet am loath to depart from my purpose."

" King Creon," said the old men, " thou needest good counsel."

" What, then, would ye have done ? "

" Set free the maiden from the sepulchre, and give this dead man burial."

Then the King cried to his people that they should bring bars wherewith to loosen the doors of the sepulchre, and hasted with them to the place. But coming on their way to the body of Prince Polynices, they took it up, and washed it, and buried that which remained of it, and raised over the ashes a great mound of earth. And this being done, they drew near to the place of the sepulchre; and as they approached, the King heard within a very piteous voice, and

THE STORY OF ANTIGONE.

knew it for the voice of his son. Then he bade his attendants loose the door with all speed; and when they had loosed it, they beheld within a very piteous sight. For the maiden Antigone had hanged herself by the girdle of linen which she wore, and the young man Prince Hæmon stood with his arms about her dead corpse, embracing it. And when the King saw him, he cried to him to come forth; but the Prince glared fiercely upon him and answered him not a word, but drew his two-edged sword. Then the King, thinking that his son was minded in his madness to slay him, leapt back, but the Prince drave the sword into his own heart, and fell forward on the earth, still holding the dead maiden in his arms. And when they brought the tidings of these things to Queen Eurydice, that was the wife of King Creon and mother to the Prince, she could not endure the grief, being thus bereaved of her children, but laid hold of a sword, and slew herself therewith.

So the house of King Creon was left desolate unto him that day, because he despised the ordinances of the Gods.

THE STORY OF IPHIGENIA IN AULIS.

KING AGAMEMNON sat in his tent at Aulis, where the army of the Greeks was gathered together, being about to sail against the great city of Troy. And it was now past midnight; but the King slept not, for he was careful and troubled about many things. And he had a lamp before him, and in his hand a tablet of pine wood, whereon he wrote. But he seemed not to remain in the same mind about that which he wrote; for now he would blot out the letters, and then would write them again; and now he fastened the seal upon the tablet and then brake it. And as he did this he wept, and was like to a man distracted. But after a while he called to an old man, his attendant (the man had been given in time past by Tyndareus to his daughter, Queen Clytæmnestra), and said—

THE STORY OF IPHIGENIA IN AULIS.

"Old man, thou knowest how Calchas the soothsayer bade me offer for a sacrifice to Artemis, who is goddess of this place, my daughter Iphigenia, saying that so only should the army have a prosperous voyage from this place to Troy, and should take the city and destroy it; and how when I heard these words I bade Talthybius the herald go throughout the army and bid them depart, every man to his own country, for that I would not do this thing; and how my brother, King Menelaüs, persuaded me so that I consented to it. Now, therefore, hearken to this, for what I am about to tell thee three men only know, namely, Calchas the soothsayer, and Menelaüs, and Ulysses, King of Ithaca. I wrote a letter to my wife the Queen, that she should send her daughter to this place, that she might be married to King Achilles; and I magnified the man to her, saying that he would in no wise sail with us unless I would give him my daughter in marriage. But now I have changed my purpose, and have written another letter after this fashion, as I will now set forth to thee,—' DAUGHTER OF LEDA, SEND NOT THY

CHILD TO THE LAND OF EUBŒA, FOR I WILL GIVE HER IN MARRIAGE AT ANOTHER TIME.'"

"Aye," said the old man, "but how wilt thou deal with King Achilles? Will he not be wroth, hearing that he hath been cheated of his wife?"

"Not so," answered the King, "for we have indeed used his name, but he knoweth nothing of this marriage. And now make haste. Sit not thou down by any fountain in the woods, and suffer not thine eyes to sleep. And beware lest the chariot bearing the Queen and her daughter pass thee where the roads divide. And see that thou keep the seal upon this letter unbroken."

So the old man departed with the letter. But scarcely had he left the tent when King Menelaüs spied him and laid hands on him, taking the letter and breaking the seal. And the old man cried out—

"Help, my lord; here is one hath taken thy letter!"

Then King Agamemnon came forth from his tent, saying, "What meaneth this uproar and disputing that I hear?"

And Menelaüs answered, "Seest thou this letter that I hold in my hand?"

"I see it: it is mine. Give it to me."

"I give it not till I have read that which is written therein to all the army of the Greeks."

"Where didst thou find it?"

"I found it while I waited for thy daughter till she should come to the camp."

"What hast thou to do with that? May I not rule my own household?"

Then Menelaüs reproached his brother because he did not continue in one mind. "For first," he said, "before thou wast chosen captain of the host, thou wast all things to all men, greeting every man courteously, and taking him by the hand, and talking with him, and leaving thy doors open to any that would enter; but afterwards, being now chosen, thou wast haughty and hard of access. And next, when this trouble came upon the army, and thou wast sore afraid lest thou shouldst lose thy office, and so miss renown, didst thou not hearken to Calchas the soothsayer, and promise thy daughter for sacrifice, and send for her to the camp, making pretence of giving her in marriage to Achilles? And now thou art gone back from thy word. Surely this is an evil day for Greece, that is troubled because thou wantest wisdom."

Then answered King Agamemnon, "What is thy quarrel with me? Why blamest thou me if thou couldst not rule thy wife? And now to win back this woman, because forsooth she is fair, thou castest aside both reason and honour. And I, if I had an ill purpose, and now have changed it for that which is wiser, dost thou charge me with folly? Let them that sware the oath to Tyndareus go with thee on this errand. Why should I slay my child, and work for myself sorrow and remorse without end that thou mayest have vengeance for thy wicked wife?"

Then Menelaüs turned away in a rage, crying, "Betray me if thou wilt. I will betake myself to other counsels and other friends."

But even as he spake there came a messenger, saying, "King Agamemnon, I am come, as thou badest me, with thy daughter Iphigenia. Also her mother, Queen Clytæmnestra, is come, bringing with her her little son, Orestes. And now they are resting themselves and their horses by the side of a spring, for indeed the way is long and weary. And all the army is gathered about them, to see them and greet them. And men question much wherefore they are come, saying, 'Doth the King make a marriage for his daughter; or hath he sent for her, desiring to see her?' But I know thy purpose, my lord; wherefore we will dance and shout and make merry, for this is a happy day for the maiden."

But the King Agamemnon was sore dismayed when he knew that the Queen was come, and spake to himself, "Now what shall I say to my wife? For that she is rightly come to the marriage of her daughter who can deny? But what will she say when she knoweth my purpose? And of the maiden, what shall I say? Unhappy maiden whose bridegroom shall be death! For she will cry to me, 'Wilt thou kill me, my father?' And the little Orestes will wail, not knowing what he doeth, seeing he is but a babe. Cursed be Paris, who hath wrought this woe!"

And now King Menelaüs came back, saying that it repented him of what he had said, "For why should thy child die for me? What hath she to do with Helen? Let the army be scattered, so that this wrong be not done."

Then said King Agamemnon, "But how shall I escape from this strait? For the whole host will compel me to this deed?"

"Not so," said King Menelaüs, "if thou wilt send back the maiden to Argos."

"But what shall that profit," said the King; "for Calchas will cause the matter to be known, or Ulysses, saying that I have failed of my promise; and if I fly to Argos, they will come and destroy my city and lay waste my land. Woe is me! in what a strait am I set! But take thou care, my brother, that Clytæmnestra hear nothing of these things."

And when he had ended speaking, the Queen herself came unto the tent, riding in a chariot, having her daughter by her side. And she bade one of the attendants take out with care the caskets which she had brought for her daughter, and bade others help her daughter to alight, and herself also, and to a fourth she said that he should take the young Orestes. Then Iphigenia greeted her father, saying, "Thou hast done well to send for me, my father."

he said that it should be in the same moon, on the first lucky day; and as to the place, that it must be where the bridegroom was sojourning, that is to say, in the camp. "And I," said the King, "will give the maiden to her husband."

"But where," answered the Queen, "is it your pleasure that I should be?"

"Thou must return to Argos, and care for the maidens there."

"Sayest thou that I must return? Who then will hold up the torch for the bride?"

"I will do that which is needful. For it is not seemly that thou shouldst be present where the whole army is gathered together."

"Aye, but it is seemly that a mother should give her daughter in marriage."

"But the maidens at home should not be left alone."

"They are well kept in their chambers."

"Be persuaded, lady."

"Not so: thou shalt order that which is without the house, but I that which is within."

But now came Achilles, to tell the King that the army was growing impatient, saying that, unless they might sail speedily to Troy, they would return each man to his home. And when the Queen heard his name—for he had said to the attendant, "Tell thy master that Achilles, the son of Peleus, would speak with him"—she came forth from the tent and greeted him, and bade him give her his right hand. And when the young man was ashamed (for it was not counted a seemly thing that men should speak with women) she said—

"But why art thou ashamed, seeing that thou art about to marry my daughter?"

And he answered, "What sayest thou, lady? I cannot speak for wonder at thy words."

"Often men are ashamed when they see new friends, and the talk is of marriage."

"But, lady, I never was suitor for thy daughter. Nor have the sons of Atreus said aught to me of the matter."

But the Queen was beyond measure astonished, and cried, "Now this is shameful indeed, that I should seek a bridegroom for my daughter in such fashion."

But when Achilles would have departed, to inquire of the King what this thing might mean, the old man that had at the first carried the letter came forth, and bade him stay. And when he had assurance that he should receive no harm for what he should tell them, he unfolded the whole matter. And when the Queen had heard it, she cried to Achilles, "O son of Thetis of the sea! help me now in this strait, and help this maiden that hath been called thy bride, though this indeed be false. 'Twill be a shame to thee if such wrong be done under thy name; for it is thy name that hath undone us. Nor have I any altar to which I may flee, nor any friend but thee only in this army."

Then Achilles made answer, "Lady, I learnt from Chiron, who was the most righteous of men, to be true and honest. And if the sons of Atreus govern according to right, I obey them; and if not, not. Know, then, that thy daughter, seeing that she hath been given, though but in word only, to me, shall not be slain by her father. For if she so die, then shall my name be brought to great dishonour, seeing that through it thou hast been persuaded to come with her to this place. This sword shall see right soon whether any one will dare to take this maiden from me."

And now King Agamemnon came forth, saying that all things were ready for the marriage, and that they waited for the maiden, not knowing that the whole matter had been revealed to the Queen. Then she said—

"Tell me now, dost thou purpose to slay thy daughter and mine?" And when he was silent, not knowing, indeed, what to say, she reproached him with many words, that she had been a loving and faithful wife to him, for which he made her an ill recompense slaying her child.

And when she had made an end of speaking, the maiden came forth from the tent, holding the young child Orestes in her arms, and cast herself upon her knees before her father, and besought him, saying, "I would, my father, that I had the voice of Orpheus, who made even the rocks to follow him, that I might persuade thee; but now all that I have I give, even these tears. O my father, I am thy child; slay me not before my time. This light is sweet to look upon. Drive me not from it to the land of darkness. I was the first to call thee father; and the first to whom thou didst say 'my child.' And thou wouldst say to me, 'Some day, my child, I shall see thee a happy wife in the home of a rich husband.' And I would answer, 'And I will receive thee with all love when thou art old, and pay thee back for all the benefits thou hast done unto me.' This I indeed remember, but thou forgettest; for thou art ready to slay me. Do it not, I beseech thee, by Pelops thy grandsire, and Atreus thy father, and this my mother, who travailed in childbirth of me, and now travaileth again in her sorrow. And thou, O my brother, though thou art but a babe, help me. Weep with me; beseech thy father that he slay not thy sister. O my father, though he be silent, yet, indeed, he beseecheth thee. For his sake, therefore, yea, and for mine own, have pity upon me, and slay me not."

But the King was sore distracted, knowing not what he should say or do, for a terrible necessity was upon him, seeing that the army could not make their journey to Troy unless this deed should first be done. And while he doubted came Achilles, saying that there was a horrible tumult in the camp, the men crying out that the maiden must be sacrificed, and that when he would have stayed them from their purpose, the people had stoned him with stones, and that his own Myrmidons helped him not; but rather were the first to assail him. Nevertheless, he said that he would fight for the maiden, even to the utmost; and that there were faithful men who would stand with him and help him. But when the maiden heard these words, she stood forth and said, "Hearken to me, my mother. Be not wroth with my father, for we cannot fight against fate. Also we must take thought that this young man suffer not, for his help will avail nought, and he himself will perish. Therefore I am resolved to die; for all Greece looketh to me; for without me the ships cannot make their voyage, nor the city of Troy be taken. Thou didst bear me, my mother, not for thyself only, but for this whole people. Wherefore I will give myself for them. Offer me for an offering; and let the Greeks take the city of Troy, for this shall be my memorial for ever."

Then said Achilles, "Lady, I should count myself most happy if the Gods would grant thee to be my wife. For I love thee well, when I see thee how noble thou art. And if thou wilt, I will carry thee to my home. And I doubt not that I shall save thee, though all the men of Greece be against me."

But the maiden answered, "What I say, I say with full purpose. Nor will I that any man should die for me, but rather will I save this land of Greece."

And Achilles said, "If this be thy will, lady, I cannot say nay, for it is a noble thing that thou doest."

Nor was the maiden turned from her purpose though her mother besought her with many tears. So they that were appointed led her to the grove of Artemis, where there was built an altar, and the whole army of the Greeks gathered about it. But when the King saw her going to her death he covered his face with his mantle; but she stood by him, and said, "I give my body with a willing heart to die for my country and for the whole land of Greece. I pray the Gods that ye may prosper, and win the victory in this war, and come back safe to your homes. And now let no man touch me, for I will offer my neck to the sword with a good heart."

And all men marvelled to see the maiden of what a good courage she was. Then the herald Talthybius stood in the midst and commanded silence to the people; and Calchas the soothsayer put a garland about her head, and drew a sharp knife from his sheath. And all the army stood regarding the maiden and the priest and the altar.

Then there befell a marvellous thing. For Calchas struck with his knife, for the sound of the stroke all men heard, but the maiden was not there. Whither she had gone no one knew; but in her stead there lay gasping a great hind, and all the altar was red with the blood thereof.

And Calchas said, "See ye this, men of Greece, how the goddess hath provided this offering in the place of the maiden, for she would not that her altar should be defiled with innocent blood. Be of good courage, therefore, and depart every man to his ship, for this day ye shall sail across the sea to the land of Troy."

But how it fared with the maiden may be read in the story of "Iphigenia among the Taurians."

THE STORY OF PHILOCTETES, OR THE BOW OF HERCULES.

Prince Philoctetes, who reigned in Methone, which is in the land of Thessaly, sailed with the other Princes of Greece to make war against the great city of Troy. For he also had been one of the suitors of Helen the Fair, and had bound himself with a great oath that he would avenge her and her husband, whomsoever she should choose, on any man that should dare to do her wrong. Now Philoctetes had been companion to Hercules in many of his labours, and also had been with him when he died upon Mount Æta. For which cause Hercules gave him the bow and the arrows which he bare, having received them at the first from Apollo. A very mighty bow it was, shooting arrows so as none other could do, and the arrows were sure dealers of death, for they had been dipped in the blood of the great dragon of Lerna, and the wounds which they made no physician might heal. But it chanced that the Prince, being on his voyage to Troy, landed at the island of Chrysa, where there was an altar of Athené, the goddess of the lace, and, desiring to show the altar to his companions, he approached it too nearly; whereupon the serpent that guarded it, lest it should be profaned, bit him in the foot. The wound was very sore and could not be healed, but tormented him day and night with grievous pains, making him groan and cry aloud. And when men were troubled with his complainings, and also with the noisome stench of his wound, the chiefs took counsel together, and it seemed good to the sons of Atreus, King Agamemnon and King Menelaüs, who were the leaders of the host, that he should be left alone on the island of Lemnos. This matter they committed to Ulysses, who did according to their bidding. But when the Greeks had laid siege to the city of Troy, nigh upon ten years, they remembered Prince Philoctetes and how they had dealt with him. For now the great Achilles was dead, having been slain by Prince Paris with an arrow in the Scæan Gate, when he was ready to break into the city; and the soothsayers affirmed that the Greeks should not have their wish upon Troy, till they should bring against it the great archer to whom they had done wrong. Then the chiefs took counsel together, and chose Ulysses, who was crafty beyond all other men, to accomplish this matter, and with him they sent Neoptolemus, the son of Achilles, who excelled in strength, even as his father had done.

Now when these two were landed upon the island, Ulysses led the way to the place where in time past he had left Philoctetes. A cave it was in the cliff, with two mouths to it, of which the one looked to the east and the other to the west, so that in winter time a man might see the sun and be warm, but in summer the wind blew through it, bringing coolness and sleep, and a little below was a spring of fair water to drink. Then said Ulysses to Neoptolemus, "Go and spy out the place, and see whether or no the man be there."

And the Prince went up and looked into the cave, and found that it was empty, but that there were signs of one who dwelt there, a bed of leaves, and a cup of wood, very rudely fashioned, and pieces of wood for kindling fires, and also, a very piteous sight, the rags wherewith the sick man was wont to dress his wound. And when he had told what he saw, Ulysses said, "That the man dwelleth here is manifest; nor can he be far away, for how can one that is wounded travel far? Doubtless he is gone to some place whither the birds resort to slay them, or, haply, to find some herb wherewith to assuage his pain. But do thou set one who will wait for his coming, for it would fare ill with me should he find me."

And when the watch had been set Ulysses said again, "I will tell what it is needful for thee to say and do. Only thou must be bold, son of Achilles, and that not only with thy hand, but in heart also, if what I shall now unfold to thee shall seem new or strange. Hearken then: when the man shall ask thee who thou art and whence thou comest, thou shalt answer him that thou art the son of Achilles, and that thou hast left the host of the Greeks, because they had done thee great wrong, for that, having prayed thee to come as not being able to take the great city of Troy without thee, yet they would not deliver to thee the arms of thy father Achilles, but gave them to Ulysses. And here thou mayest speak against me all kinds of evil, for such words will not trouble me, but if thou accomplish not this thing thou wilt trouble the whole host of the Greeks. For know that without this man's bow thou canst not take the city of Troy; know also that thou only canst approach him without peril, not being of the number of those who sailed with him at the first. And if it please thee not to get the bow by stealth, for this indeed thou must do—and I know thee to be one that loveth not to speak falsely or to contrive deceit—yet bethink thee that victory is sweet. Be thou bold to-day, and we will be righteous to-morrow."

Then the Prince made reply, " 'Tis not in me, son of Laertes, to work by craft and guile, neither was it in my father before me. I am ready to carry off this man with a strong arm; and how, being a cripple, shall he stand against us? but deceit I will not use. And though I should be loath to fail thee in this our common enterprise, yet were this better than to prevail by fraud."

Then said Ulysses, "And I, too, in my youth would do all things by the hand and not by the tongue; but now I know that the tongue hath alone the mastery."

And the Prince replied, " But thou biddest me speak the thing that is false."

" I bid thee prevail over Philoctetes by craft."

" But why may I not persuade him, or even constrain him by force ? "

" To persuasion he will not hearken, and force thou mayest not use, for he hath arrows that deal death without escape."

" But is it not a base thing for a man to lie ? "

" Surely not, if a lie save him."

" Tell me what is the gain to me if this man come to Troy."

" Without this bow and these arrows Troy falleth not. For though it is the pleasure of the Gods that thou take the city, yet canst not thou take it without these, nor indeed these without thee."

And when the Prince had mused awhile, he said, "If this be so with the arms, I must needs get them."

Then Ulysses said, " Do this, and thou shalt gain a double honour."

And the Prince said, "What meanest thou

by thy 'double honour'? Tell me, and I refuse no more."

"The praise of wisdom and of courage also."

"Be it so: I will do this deed, nor count it shame."

"'Tis well," said Ulysses, "and now I will despatch this watcher to the ship, whom I will send again in pilot's disguise if thou desire, and it seems needful. Also I myself will depart, and may Hermes, the god of craft, and Athené, who ever is with me, cause us to prevail."

After a while Philoctetes came up the path to the cave very slowly, and with many groans. And when he saw the strangers (for now some of the ship's crew were with Prince Neoptolemus) he cried, "Who are ye that are come to this inhospitable land? Greeks I know you to be by your garb; but tell me more."

And when the Prince had told his name and lineage, and that he was sailing from Troy, Philoctetes cried, "Sayest thou from Troy? Yet surely thou didst not sail with us in the beginning."

"What?" cried the Prince. "Hadst thou then a share in this matter of Troy?"

And Philoctetes made reply, "Knowest thou not whom thou seest? Hast thou not heard the story of my sorrows?" And when he heard that the young man knew nothing of these things: "Surely this is sorrow upon sorrow if no report of my state hath come to the land of Greece, and I lie here alone, and my disease groweth upon me, but my enemies laugh and keep silence!" And then he told his name and fortunes, and how the Greeks had left him on the shore while he slept, and how it was the tenth year of his sojourning in the island. "For know," he said, "that it is without haven or anchorage, and no man cometh hither of his free will; and if any come unwilling, as indeed it doth sometimes chance, they speak soft words to me and give me, haply, some meat; but when I make suit to them that they carry me to my home, they will not. And this wrong the sons of Atreus and Ulysses have worked against me; for which may the Gods who dwell in Olympus make them equal recompense."

"And I," said the Prince, "am no lover of these men. For when Achilles was dead——"

"How sayest thou? Is the son of Peleus dead?"

"Yea; but it was the hand of a God and not of a man that slew him."

"A mighty warrior slain by a mighty foe! But say on."

"Ulysses, and Phœnix who was my sire's foster-father, came in a ship to fetch me; and when I was come to the camp they even greeted me kindly, and sware that it was Achilles' self they saw, so like was I to my sire. And, my mourning ended, I sought the sons of Atreus and asked of them the arms of my father, but they made answer that they had given them to Ulysses; and Ulysses, chancing to be there, affirmed that they had done well, seeing that he had saved them from the enemy. And when I could prevail nothing, I sailed away in great wrath."

"'Tis even," Philoctetes made reply, "as I should have judged of them. But I marvel that the Greater Ajax endured to see such doings."

"Ah! but he was already dead."

"This is grievous news. And how fares old Nestor of Pylos?"

"But ill, for his eldest born, Antilochus, is dead."

"I could have spared any rather than these two, Ajax and Antilochus. But Patroclus, where was he when thy father died?"

"He was already slain. For 'tis ever thus that war taketh the true man and leaveth the false. But of these things I have had enough and more than enough. Henceforth my island of Scyros, though it be rocky and small, shall content me. And now, Prince Philoctetes, I go, for the wind favours us, and we must take the occasion which the Gods give us."

And when Philoctetes knew that Neoptolemus was about to depart, he besought him with many prayers that he would take him also on his ship; for the voyage, he said, would not be of more than a single day. "Put me," he said, "where thou wilt, in forecastle, or hold, or stern, and set me on shore even as it may seem best to thee. Only take me from this place." And the sailors also made entreaty to the Prince that he would do so; and he, after a while, made as if he consented to their prayers.

But while Philoctetes was yet thanking him

and his companions, there came two men to the cave, of whom one was a sailor in the Prince's ship, and the other a merchant. And the merchant said that he was sailing from Troy to his home, and that chancing to come to the island, and knowing that the Prince was there, he judged it well to tell him his news; 'twas briefly this, that Phœnix and the sons of Theseus had sailed, having orders from the sons of Atreus that they should bring the Prince back; and also that Ulysses and Diomed were gone on another errand, even to fetch some one of whom the rulers had need. And when the Prince would know who he might be, the merchant bade him say who it was standing near, and when he heard that it was Philoctetes, he cried, "Haste thee to thy ship, son of Achilles, for this is the very man whom the two are coming to fetch. Haply thou hast not heard what befell at Troy. There is a certain Helenus, son of King Priam, and a famous soothsayer. Him Ulysses, the man of craft, took a prisoner, and brought into the assembly of Greeks; and the man prophesied to them that they should never take the city of Troy, unless they should bring thither the Prince Philoctetes from the island whereon he dwelt. And Ulysses said, 'If I bring not the man, whether willing or unwilling, then cut off my head.'"

And when Philoctetes heard this his anger was very great, and he became yet more eager to depart. But first he must go into the cave and fetch such things as he needed, herbs with which he was wont to soothe the pains of his wounds, and all the furniture of his bow. And when he spake of the bow, the Prince asked whether it was indeed the famous bow of Hercules that he carried in his hand, and would fain, he said, touch it, if only it were lawful so to do. And Philoctetes answered, "Yes, thou shalt touch it and handle it, which, indeed, no other man hath ever done, for thou hast done a good deed to me, and it was for a good deed that I myself also received it."

But when they would have gone towards the ship, the pangs of his wound came upon Philoctetes. And then at first he cried, saying, that it was well with him; but at the last, he could endure no more, and cried to the Prince that he should draw his sword and smite off the foot, nor heed if he should slay him; only he would be rid of the pain. And then he bade him take the bow and keep it for him while he slept, for that sleep came ever upon him after these great pains. Only he must keep it well, especially if those two, Ulysses and Diomed, should chance to come in the meanwhile. And when the Prince had promised this, Philoctetes gave him the bow, saying, "Take it, my son, and pray to the jealous Gods that it bring not sorrow to thee as it hath brought sorrow to me, and to him that was its master before me."

And after a while the sick man slept. And the Prince, with the sailors that were his companions, watched by him the while.

But when the sailors would have had the Prince depart, seeing that he had now the great bow and the arrows, for whose sake he had come, he would not, for they would be of no avail, he said, without the archer himself. And in no long space of time the sick man woke. Right glad was he to see that the strangers had not departed, for, indeed, he had scarce hoped that this might be. Therefore commending the young man much for his courage and loving kindness, he would have him help him straightway to the ship, that his pain having now ceased awhile, they might be ready to depart without delay. So they went, but the Prince was sorely troubled in his mind and cried, "Now what shall I do?" and "now am I at my wits' end so that even words fail me." At which words, indeed, Philoctetes was grieved, thinking that it repented the Prince of his purpose, so that he said, "Doth the trouble of my disease then hinder thee from taking me in thy ship?"

Then said the Prince, "All is trouble when a man leaveth his nature to do things that are not fitting."

And Philoctetes made answer, "Nay, is not this a fitting thing, seeing of what sire thou art the son, to help a brave man in his trouble?"

"Can I endure to be so base," said the Prince, "hiding that which I should declare, and speaking the thing that is false?" And while Philoctetes still doubted whether he repented not of his purpose, he cried aloud, "I will hide the thing no longer. Thou shalt sail with me to Troy."

"What sayest thou?"

"I say that thou shalt be delivered from these pains, and shalt prevail together with me over the great city of Troy."

"What treachery is this? What hast thou done to me? Give me back the bow."

"Nay, that I cannot do, for I am under authority, and must needs obey."

And when Philoctetes heard these words, he cried with a very piteous voice, "What a marvel of wickedness thou art that hast done this thing. Art thou not ashamed to work such wrong to a suppliant? Give me my bow, for it is my life. But I speak in vain, for he goeth away and heedeth me not. Hear me then, ye waters and cliffs, and ye beasts of the field, who have been long time my wonted company, for I have none else to hearken to me. Hear what the son of Achilles hath done to me. For he sware that he would carry me to my home, and lo! he taketh me to Troy. And he gave me the right hand of fellowship, and now he robbeth me of the bow, the sacred bow of Hercules. Nay— for I will make trial of him once more—give back this thing to me and be thy true self.

What sayest thou? Nothing? Then am I undone. O cavern of the rock wherein I have dwelt, behold how desolate I am! Never more shall I slay with my arrows bird of the air or beast of the field; but that which I hunted shall pursue me, and that on which I fed shall devour me."

And the Prince was cut to the heart when he heard these words, hating the thing which he had done, and cursing the day on which he had come from Scyros to the plains of Troy. Then turning himself to the sailors, he asked what he should do, and was even about to give back the bow, when Ulysses, who was close at hand, watching what should be done, ran forth crying that he should hold his hand.

Then said Philoctetes, "Is this Ulysses that I see? Then am I undone."

"'Tis even so: and as for what thou askest of this youth, that he should give back the bow, he shall not do it; but rather thou shalt sail with us to Troy; and if thou art not willing, these that stand by shall take thee by force."

"Lord of fire, that rulest this land of Lemnos, hearest thou this?"

"Nay, 'tis Zeus that is master here, and Zeus hath commanded this deed."

"What lies are these? Thou makest the Gods false as thyself."

"Not so. They are true and I also. But this journey thou must take."

"Methinks I am a slave, and not freeborn, that thou talkest thus."

"Thou art peer to the bravest, and with them shalt take the great city of Troy."

"Never; I had sooner cast myself down from this cliff."

Then Ulysses cried to the men that they should lay hold on him; and this they straightway did. Then Philoctetes in many words reproached him with all the wrongs that he had done; how at the first he had caused him to be left on this island, and now had stolen his arms, not with his own hands, indeed, but with craft and deceit, serving himself of a simple youth, who knew not but to do as he was bidden. And he prayed to the Gods that they would avenge him on all that had done him wrong, and chiefly on this man Ulysses.

Then Ulysses made reply, "I can be all things

as occasion serveth ; such as thou sayest, if need be ; and yet no man more pious if the time call for goodness and justice. One thing only I must needs do, and that is to prevail. Yet here I will yield to thee. Thou wilt not go ; so be it. Loose him ! We need thee not, having these arms of thine. Teucer is with us, an archer not one whit less skilful than thou. And now I leave thee to this Lemnos of thine. May be this bow shall bring me the honour which thou refusest."

When he had thus spoken he departed, and the Prince Neoptolemus with him. Only the Prince gave permission to the sailors that they should tarry with the sick man till it was time to make ready for the voyage.

Then Philoctetes bewailed himself, crying to his bow, " O my bow, my beloved, that they have wrested from my hands, surely, if thou knowest aught, thou grievest to see that the man who was the comrade of Hercules will never hold thee more, but that base hands will grasp thee, mixing thee with all manner of deceit." And then again he called to the birds of the air and the beasts of the field, that they should not fly from him any more, seeing that he had now no help against them, but should come and avenge themselves upon him and devour him. And still the sailors would have comforted him. Also they sought to persuade him that he should listen to the chiefs; but he would not, crying that the lightning should smite him before he would go to Troy and help them that had done him such wrong. And at the last he cried that they should give him a spear or a sword, that he might be rid of his life.

But while they thus talked together, the Prince came back like one that is in haste, with Ulysses following him, who cried, "Wherefore turnest thou back?"

"To undo what I did amiss."

"How sayest thou? When didst thou thus?"

"When I listened to thee, and used deceit to a brave man."

"What wilt thou then? (I fear me much what this fool may do.)"

"I will give back this bow and these arrows to him from whom I took them by craft."

"That shalt thou not do."

"But who shall hinder me?"

"That will I, and all the sons of the Greeks with me."

"This is idle talk for a wise man as thou art."

"Seest thou this sword whereto I lay my hand?"

"If thou talkest of swords, thou shalt see right soon that I also have a sword."

"Well—I let thee alone. To the host will I tell this matter; they shall judge thee."

"Now thou speakest well; be ever as wise; so shalt thou keep thy foot out of trouble."

Then the Prince called to Philoctetes, who, being loosed by the sailors, had hidden himself in the cave, and asked of him again whether he were willing to sail with him, or were resolved to abide in the island.

And when the man had denied that he would go, and had begun again to call down a curse on the sons of Atreus, and on Ulysses, and on the Prince himself, then the Prince bade him stay his speech, and gave him back the bow and the arrows.

And when Ulysses, seeing this deed, was very wroth, and threatened vengeance, Philoctetes put an arrow to the string, and drew the bow to the full, and would have shot at the man, but the Prince stayed his hand.

And then again the Prince was urgent with him that he should cease from his anger, and should sail with him to Troy, saying that there he should be healed by the great physician, the son of Asclepius, and should also win great glory by taking the city, and that right soon; for that the soothsayer Helenus had declared that it was the will of the Gods that the city of Troy should be taken that same summer.

But for all this he prevailed nothing; for Philoctetes was obstinate that he would not go to Troy, nor do any pleasure to the chiefs who had done him such wrong. But he would that the Prince should fulfil the promise which he had made, that he would carry him in his ship to his own country. And this the Prince said that he would do.

And now the two were about to depart to the ship, when lo! there appeared in the air above their heads the great Hercules. Very wonderful was he to behold, with bright raiment, and a great glory shining from his face, even as the everlasting Gods beheld him with whom he dwelt in the place of Olympus. And Hercules spake, saying—

"Go not yet, son of Pœas, before thou hearest what I shall say to thee. For 'tis Hercules whom thou seest and hearest; and I am come from my dwelling in heaven to declare to thee the will of Zeus. Know then that even as I attained to this blessedness after much toil, so shall it be with thee. For thou shalt go to the land of Troy; and first thou shalt be healed of thy grievous sickness, and afterwards thou shalt slay Paris with thine arrows, and shalt take the city of Troy, whereof thou shalt carry the spoils to thy home, even to Pœas thy father, having received from thy fellows the foremost prize for valour. But remember that all that thou winnest in this warfare thou must take as an offering to my tomb. And to thee, son of Achilles, I say; thou canst not take the city of Troy without this man, nor he without thee. Whereof, as two lions that consort together, guard ye each other. And I will send Asclepius to heal him of his sickness; for it is the will of the Gods that Troy should yet again be taken by my bow. And remember this, when ye lay waste the land, to have the Gods and that which belongeth to them in reverence."

Then said Philoctetes, "O my master, whom I have long desired to hear and see, I will do as thou sayest."

And the Prince also gave his consent.

Then Philoctetes bade farewell to the island in these words—

> "Home that hast watched with me, farewell!
> And nymphs that haunt the springs or dwell
> In seaward meadows, and the roar
> Of waves that break upon the shore;
> Where often, through the cavern's mouth,
> The drifting of the rainy South
> Hath coldly drenched me as I lay;
> And Hermes' hill, whence many a day,
> When anguish seized me, to my cry
> Hoarse-sounding echo made reply.
> O fountains of the land, and thou,
> Pool of the Wolf, I leave you now;
> Beyond all hope I leave thy strand,
> O Lemnos, sea-encircled land!
> Grant me with favouring winds to go
> Whither the mighty Fates command,
> And this dear company of friends,
> And mastering Powers who shape our ends
> To issues fairer than we know."

THE STORY OF THE DEATH OF AGAMEMNON.

On the roof of King Agamemnon's palace in Argos a watchman sat watching. So had he sat night after night, through a whole year, nor was there one of the stars of heaven which he had not seen to rise and set. And as he watched, his eyes were fixed ever on the north, looking for the signal of fire which should bring good tidings to the Queen and to all Argos. For now the great city of Troy was tottering to its fall, and the ten years' toil was coming to an end.

And lo! even as it drew towards morning, there was a light in the sky that was not the light of the sun, and the man cried aloud, 'Now blessed be this light that I have watched for, seeing that it bringeth good tidings to this land. I will straightway to the Queen that she send the news about the city. And may

the Gods grant that I join hand to hand with
my master when he cometh back to his home,
wherein if there be aught that is ill-ordered,
who am I that I should speak thereof? Let
the walls cry out, if they will, only I will keep
silence."

Then he made haste and told the Queen,
who sent messengers throughout Argos, bidding
that men should burn thank-offerings of
incense on every altar. Also she would that
the old men, who were the chiefs and counsellors
of the city, should be gathered together
to the palace, that they might know the truth
of the matter. And while they waited for the
Queen, they talked much of what had been in
days gone by, in the beginning of the ten
years' war, when King Agamemnon, with King
Menelaüs, who was his brother, sailed from
that very land of Argos, seeking vengeance for
Queen Helen. And one said, "Remember ye
not what we saw when the army set forth from
the city? how upon the right hand as they
marched there appeared two eagles, one black
altogether and the other with feathers of white
in him, that devoured a hare big with young

ones? and how Calchas, the soothsayer, interpreted the thing, saying, 'The eagles are the two kings; and as these have devoured the hare, so shall the kings devour the city of Troy together with her children! Only we must needs pray that there come not wrath upon the army. For Queen Artemis loveth not these winged dogs of her father Zeus, even the eagles. And if her anger be kindled against us, we shall not turn it away save by an evil sacrifice, from which also shall spring great wrath in the time to come. Therefore may Apollo help us, who is the healer of all evils.' So spake Calchas, the soothsayer, knowing indeed that Queen Artemis was wroth with King Agamemnon, for that he had hunted and slain, even in her own grove, a beautiful hart which she loved."

Then said another of the elders, "Nor indeed did the wrath of the goddess tarry. For when the army was gathered together in Aulis she caused that the winds blew ever from the north and hindered the ships from their voyage, so that the men were pinched with hunger and wasted with disease. Then said Calchas, the soothsayer, 'This is the thing whereof I spake: the goddess asketh the sacrifice that thou knowest of.' But when the kings heard this, they wept, and smote with their sceptres upon the ground. And King Agamemnon said, 'How shall I do this thing, and slay my own daughter, even Iphigenia, who is the joy and beauty of my dwelling? Yet it were base to be false to them that have trusted me to be their leader in this war. Therefore the Gods shall have their will.' Thus he hardened his heart to the evil work; nor did the chiefs have pity on her for all that she was young and fair exceedingly. So when the priests had ended their prayers, her father bade the ministers take her as she lay with her robes about her, and lift her up on the altar, even as men lift a kid which they slay for sacrifice, putting a bridle upon her lips, that she should not cry aloud. Then she let fall to the earth her saffron veil, being fair to see as a very lovely picture, and smote all that stood by with a look exceeding piteous: yea, and would fain have spoken to them, for often had they heard her voice when she sang in the guest-hall of her father. But of the end what

DEATH OF AGAMEMNON. 143

need to speak? Who knoweth it not? For indeed the counsels of Calchas were fulfilled."

While they talked these things one to another the Queen Clytæmnestra came forth from the palace, and they asked her, "Hast thou heard good news, O Queen, that thou biddest them burn incense on the altars?"

"Good news, indeed," she said, "for the Greeks have taken the great city of Troy."

And when they doubted if this could be so, and would know when the thing had happened, and how she had heard it so speedily, she set the matter forth to them, as the king had ordered it. "For first," she said, "they made a great fire on Mount Ida, which is over Troy; and from Ida the light passed to the island of Lemnos, and from Lemnos to the mountain of Athos. But Athos sent it on southward across the sea, on a path of gold like the sunshine, even to Makistus in Eubœa, and Makistus to Messapius, and Messapius, kindling a great pile of heath, sent it, bright as is the moon, across the plain of the Asopus to the cliffs of Cithæron. And from Cithæron it travelled, brighter than before, by the lake Gorgopis to the hill of Ægiplanctus, which looketh down upon the Saronic gulf, and hence to Arachneüs, which is hard by the city. Thus hath the King sent the tidings to me."

"Tell us more," said the old man, "for we can scarcely believe this thing."

"Of a truth," said the Queen, "this day the Greeks possess the city of Troy, wherein, I trow, are many things which ill agree. For women are making lamentation for husbands and brothers slain with the sword, while the conquerors feast and live softly, being quit of hunger and cold and watchings. Only let them do honour to the gods of the city, nor lay hands greedy of gain on that which is holy. So shall they have a safe return. But if they anger the Gods, haply there shall come upon them the vengeance of them that are slain."

Then the Queen departed, and the old men spake again among themselves. "Now are the sinners, the men of Troy, caught in the net of destruction! Long since did Zeus bend the bow and make it ready against the transgressor, and now hath the arrow sped to the mark! Evil was the day when Paris shamed the table of

DEATH OF AGAMEMNON.

his host, stealing the wife of his bosom! Evil the hour when she went, as one that goeth lightly and carelessly, through the gates of Troy, and brought with her the dowry of destruction and death. Sorrow she left behind her in her home; the desolate couch and the empty hall, for here, the grace of the shapely statues mocked her husband's grief with the stony stare of their loveless eyes, and there, but the empty joy remained that dwells in the dreams of the night. Aye! and a sorrow she left that was greater than this. For the heroes went forth from the land of Greece, valiant and wise and true; and lo! all that Ares, the changer, but not of money, sendeth back is a handful of ashes shut in an urn of brass! Therefore there is wrath in the city against the sons of Atreus, the leaders of the host; nor does the vengeance of the Gods forget the shedder of blood."

But while they talked thus among themselves, some yet doubting whether the thing were true, cried one of them, "Now shall we know the certainty of this matter, for here cometh a herald with leaves of olive on his head, and he hath dust on his garments and mire on his feet, as one who cometh from a journey."

Then the herald, whose name was Talthybius, came to the place where they had assembled, and when he had saluted Zeus and Apollo, whom, having been an enemy at Troy, he would fain have as friend, and Hermes, who was the god of his heralds' craft, he said, " Know ye all that King Agamemnon hath come, having, by the help of Zeus, executed judgment to the full against Troy and her children, for the evil which they wrought against the Gods and against this land."

Then he told the elders what things they had suffered, first on sea, being crowded together on shipboard ; and then on land, having their lodging near to the walls of their enemies, and under the open canopy of heaven, being drenched with rains and dews, and frozen with snows from Mount Ida, and burnt with the sun in the windless days of summer. " But now," he said, " these things are past and gone. And we will nail the spoils of Troy in the temples of the Gods, to be a memorial for them that shall come after. But let the people rejoice, and praise their King and his captains."

Then came forth Queen Clytæmnestra, and said, "Mark ye who doubted, how that all things are even as I said. And now, herald, go tell thy lord that I wait to receive him with all honour; wherefore let him come with what speed he may; so shall he find a faithful guardian in his house who hath kept true watch and ward over all that he left behind, for this is the boast I make, both true and well beseeming a noble dame."

Then said the chief of the elders, "Listen to her, herald, for her words are fair. But tell me now, hath Menelaüs had safe return?"

"Would," said he, "I had some better thing to tell! But what profiteth it to deceive? Truly, the man, together with his ship, is vanished out of our sight."

"Sailed he then before you?" said the elder, "or was he parted from you in a storm?"

"'Twas even so," answered the herald.

"And did men judge of him as living or dead?"

"That, indeed, no man knoweth, but only

the sun who seeth all things. But hearken, I will declare the whole matter. There went out wrath from heaven against us. For after we had set sail, the waves rose high in the night, and the fierce winds from the north dashed our ships one against another, so that when the morning came, lo! the sea was covered with bodies of men and wrecks. But the ship of the King suffered not, for the hand of a god, I trow, and not of a man, held the helm. But be of good cheer. For doubtless they too think of us as of those that have perished, even as we of them. And as for Menelaüs, be assured that he will yet return, for the will of Zeus is not that this house should perish."

Then said one of the old men, "Rightly they named her Helen, for like *hell* hath she devoured men and ships, aye, and this great city of Troy. I have heard tell how a man reared a lion's cub in his house. Very pleasant was he at the first, for the children played with him, and he made sport for the old; but when he grew he showed the temper of his race, and filled the house with blood. Even so came Helen, smiling and fair, to Troy, and now behold the end! But here cometh King Agamemnon. Let us greet him in fitting fashion."

And as he spake the King came near to the doors of the palace, sitting in a chariot drawn by mules; and by him sat Cassandra, who was daughter to King Priam, having been given to him by the princes when they divided the spoil of Troy. And when the King had saluted the Gods, giving them thanks that they had helped him to take vengeance on the men of Troy, and had also set forth his purpose to order all things in a regular assembly if anything had been done amiss in his absence, there came forth the Queen to greet him, saying, " I am not ashamed, men of Argos, to confess that with great gladness of heart I receive my husband. For truly it is an evil lot for a woman when she sitteth alone in her house, hearing continually rumours and tidings of misfortune. Verily, had my lord here been wounded as oft as fame related this thing of him, these same wounds had been more in number than the meshes of a net; and had he died as often as men reported him dead, three bodies such as the story telleth Geryon to have had, had not sufficed him.

Hence it is, O King, that our son Orestes is not here, for I sent him to Strophius the Phocian, who is, as thou knowest, an ancient friend of our house, fearing, if aught should befall thee at Troy, lest some tumult of the people should work harm also unto him. Scant truly and light have been my slumbers, and with many tears have I watched for thee. And now thou art come, what shall I say? Truly this man is to me as the strong pillar of a roof, as an only child to a father, as land seen beyond all hope by sailors, after much toil at sea, as a clear shining after storm, as a fountain springing forth to one that journeyeth in a thirsty land. And now, my lord, I would that thou step from thy car, not setting thy foot upon the earth, seeing that it hath trampled upon the great city of Troy. Why linger ye, ye maids? Strew the pathway with carpeting of purple!"

And King Agamemnon made answer, "Truly, daughter of Leda, thy speech hath been even as my absence, exceeding long. But why dost thou pamper me with luxury, or make my goings hateful to the Gods, strewing this purple under my feet? It is not well, me thinks, that a man should trample on such wealth."

"Nay," said the Queen, "be content. Thinkest thou that Priam would not have walked on purple if perchance he had been the conqueror?"

And after they had talked awhile, she prevailed, only the King bade them loose the sandals from under his feet, thinking it shame to waste the substance of his house. Also he gave commandment that they should deal very kindly with the strange woman that had ridden with him in his chariot, for that the Gods have a favour unto them that use their victory with mercy. And when he had said these things he went into the palace, the Queen leading the way.

Then one of the elders said, "There is a nameless fear in my heart; and when I should rejoice for the return of the King and the host, a voice of boding riseth to my lips. If a man be wealthy above measure, let him fling overboard a part, and so escape shipwreck of his house. But blood that hath been spilt upon the earth, what charmer can bring back? Did not Zeus slay the man who raised the dead? For a while 'twere best to be silent."

Then the Queen came forth from the palace, and bade Cassandra descend from the car and enter the gates. For why, she said, should she struggle against fate which made her to be a slave? Happy indeed was the lot which had brought her to a house of ancient wealth. 'Twas the newly rich that used harshness to their slaves. But her persuasion availed nothing with the maiden, for she sat and made no answer; and though the old men joined their counsel to the same end, she moved not nor spake. But when the Queen was departed again into the palace, she began to cry aloud, like unto one that was possessed, that there came a smell from the house, as the smell of a slaughter-house, and that she saw the shapes of children who had been cruelly murdered; and then, that another crime was now about to be wrought, a bath made ready, and an entangling robe, and a double-headed axe lifted to strike. And then she spake of herself, that the doom was upon her, and that the King had brought her to die with him, and that she should fall even as the city of her father had fallen. But after awhile her fury abated, and she began to speak plainly. And first she told the elders how

DEATH OF AGAMEMNON. 153

it came to pass that she had this gift of prophecy, that she could see what had been, as indeed she had spoken of ancient wickedness that had been done in the house, and also could tell beforehand what should come hereafter. For that Apollo had loved her, and had given her this art; but, because she had deceived him, he had added thereto this curse, that no one should believe her even speaking truth. And then she told them that the old crimes of the house should end in yet another crime; that there was one in the house, a woman to look at, but in truth a very Scylla, a monster of the sea. And at the last she declared plainly that they should see the King Agamemnon lying dead. But the curse was upon her, and they believed her not. And then crying out that she saw a lioness that had taken a wolf to be her paramour, she cast away the tokens of prophecy that she carried, the staff from her hand, and the necklace from about her neck. And when she had done this she went to the palace gates, knowing that she went to her death. But first she said that there should come an avenger who should execute vengeance for his father that had been slain and also for her. And when she was arrived at the door of the palace, at the first she started back, for the smell of blood smote her in the face; but then she took heart again and passed on. Only first she turned and said, "O Sun, whose light I see now for the last time, grant that the hand that taketh vengeance for the King may take it also for the slave-woman whom they slay—a conquest, in good sooth, right easy to be made."

But while the old men doubted what these things might mean, saying that no man could trust in prosperous fortune, if the King, who had won such a victory over the city of Troy, should himself perish, there came a dreadful voice from within, crying out, "Woe is me! I am smitten with a mortal blow!" And while they doubted, it came again, crying, "Woe again! I am smitten with a second blow!" Then they debated what were best to do; and one would have them call to the citizens for help, and another that they should rush into the palace; and some doubted whether aught might now avail. And lo! the great doors of the palace were thrown back and there appeared a dreadful sight — two dead bodies, covered each with a veil, and the Queen, with an axe in her hand, standing beside them, who said—

"I spake before words fitting the time, and now I am not ashamed to speak that which is contrary to them. For this is in truth an old purpose that I have executed. Yea, from the day that he shed the innocent blood, even the blood of Iphigenia, my daughter, it hath been in my heart to slay him. I threw a net about him, whence there was no escape, entangling his limbs in a royal robe. Twice I smote him; twice he groaned, stretching out his limbs in death; aye, and a third blow I added—my offering of thanks to the Ruler of the dead. Right glad was I when the blood spirted on me; glad as the seed when the increase-giving rain cometh down from the sky."

Then the old men, the counsellors of the city, cried shame upon her that she had done so foul a deed, saying that the people should curse her and cast her out. But she was not one whit fearful or ashamed, saying that he whom she had slain was a man of blood, and unfaithful, and that he had suffered a just punishment together with his paramour. And when they made lamentation over the King that he had been treacherously slain, she said, "Think not that I am this dead man's wife, as indeed I seem to be; rather am I the avenger that executeth judgment for the ancient evils of this house."

And when they cried, "O my King, who shall do thee due honour at thy burial, and speak thy praise, and weep for thee?" she made reply, "Trouble not yourselves with these things. As I slew him so will I bury him. And though many tears follow him not from his house, yet doubtless when he cometh to the dwellings of the dead, Iphigenia, his daughter, whom he loved, will meet him, and throw her arms about him, and kiss him, so dear a father he was to her."

And while they talked thus with each other, there came foward the Prince Ægisthus, with his guard about him, boasting that now the wrongs of his father Thyestes were avenged. Then again the strife of words grew fierce, for the counsellors reproached the Prince that he was treacherous, having bound himself with a false woman against his lord the King; and cowardly also and base, in that he had not dared to do this deed himself, but had left it to the hands of another; also they prophesied that Orestes should come and execute the just judgment of the Gods on them that had slain his father. And the Prince endured not to hear such words, but threatened bonds and imprisonment. So had strife nearly begun, for Ægisthus called to his guards, and the counsellors would fain have roused the citizens, but the Queen, for indeed she would that the shedding of blood should have an end, spake and soothed the anger of the Prince, saying, "Heed not what these babblers say. Thou and I are rulers in this place, aye, and will order all things aright."

So the two lived together for a while in great pride and joy. But the blood cried against them from the ground, and the Gods forgat them not.

THE STORY OF ELECTRA, OR THE RETURN OF ORESTES.

WHEN King Agamemnon was slain by his wicked wife Clytæmnestra, the boy Orestes his son had perished also by the hands of his mother, but that his sister Electra took him and delivered him out of the hands of them that would have slain him. And having saved him, she sent him to the house of Strophius the Phocian, who was a friend to the house of the King, her father. And here Orestes abode till he was of age and strength to fulfil the law. For the law of the land was that, if a man should be foully slain, his son should avenge him on him that had done this wrong. Also the youth sought counsel of Apollo at his oracle of Delphi, and the god answered him that he should avenge the blood of his father even upon her

THE STORY OF ELECTRA. 159

that bare him. Therefore, being now grown to manhood, he came to the city of Argos, having disguised himself that no man might know him. And he had with him Pylades that was the son of Strophius. Now these two loved each other exceedingly, so that men spake of them in after time as famous among friends. Also there came with Orestes an old man, a slave that had waited on him from a boy. Now the three had devised a story wherewith they might deceive the Queen and her husband; and being thus prepared they came into the city at dawn.

Then the old man spake, saying, "Son of Agamemnon, thou seest the city which thou hast long desired to see. There is the grove of Io, whom the gad-fly drave over the earth, and there on the left hand the temple of Heré, which all men know, and before us the palace of the children of Pelops, a house of many woes, from which I carried thee forth in time past, when thy mother would have slain thee. But now we must take counsel and that speedily, for the sun is risen and hath wakened the birds, and we must be ready before that men come forth to their work."

Then Orestes made reply, "'Tis well said, old man. Hearken then to what I purpose. And first know that when I would hear from Apollo at his oracle in Delphi how I should best avenge my father, he bade me trust neither in shield nor spear, but accomplish the deed by craft. Do thou then go when occasion shall offer into the palace, and spy out the things that are therein. For they will not know thee who thou art, so changed art thou. And thou shalt tell them such a tale about me as shall surely deceive them. And we meanwhile will do honor to the spirit of my father at his grave, offering hair that has been shorn from my head and drink offerings, and afterwards will return and accomplish what shall remain to be done."

And when he had so spoken, he prayed, "O my country and ye gods of the land, help me, and thou house of my father which I have come at the bidding of the Gods to cleanse from the guilt of blood."

Then the old man said, "I hear the voice of some one that groans." And Orestes made answer, "Doubtless it is my sister Electra. Shall we stay and listen to her?" "Not so," said the old man, "let us do our business without delay." So they departed.

And then came forth Electra, making great lamentation for her father, and praying that the Gods would speedily send her brother Orestes to avenge him. And with her was a company of the daughters of Argos, who sought to comfort her, saying that it was idle to make such weeping and moaning for the dead; and that others also were in like case with her; and that she should have patience, for that time would bring punishment on the evildoers. Also they would have her curb her tongue, seeing how she angered those that had the rule in her house.

And then Electra unfolded her grief to them saying, "I pray you, daughters of Argos, that ye think no evil of me as of one that altogether wanteth wisdom and patience. For what woman of the better sort would not do even as I? For think how I am constrained to live with them that slew my father; and that every day I see this base Ægisthus sitting upon that which was his throne, and wearing the selfsame robes; and how he is husband to this mother of mine, if indeed she be a mother who can stoop to such vileness. And know that every month on the day on which she slew my father she maketh festival and offereth sacrifice to the Gods. And all this am I constrained to see, weeping in secret, for indeed it is not permitted to me publicly to show such sorrow as my heart desireth. Ofttimes indeed this woman mocketh me, and would know why I sorrow more than others, seeing that others also have lost their fathers. But sometimes, if it so chance that she hear from some one that Orestes prepareth to come back to this land, she is furious above measure, and rageth as a wild beast; and her husband, this coward that maketh war against women, stirreth up her fury against me. And still do I look for Orestes when he shall come; but he tarrieth long, and in the meantime I perish with sorrow and trouble."

Then the daughters of Argos, when they had made inquiry and heard that Ægisthus was absent and that they could speak more freely of these matters, would fain know whether she had heard news of her brother Orestes, and bade her be of good heart concerning him. But as they spake together, the sister of Electra,

Chrysothemis, came forth with offerings for the tomb of her father in her hand, and other maidens followed her. Now these two were different one from the other, for Electra was full of courage, and would have no peace with those whom she hated, and sought not to hide what was in her heart, but Chrysothemis was fearful, and would live peaceably with them that she loved not, and would speak them fair. And now, when Electra saw her sister come forth, she brake out against her with many angry words, saying that she did ill to choose the part of a mother who had done such wickedness, and to forget her father; and that it was a base thing in her to live softly and at ease, consorting with the evildoers.

And when the Argive maidens would have made peace between them, Chrysothemis answered, "These words are not strange to me; nor should I take note of them, but that I have heard of a great trouble that is ready to fall upon my sister here, and stay her complaints even for ever."

"Nay, what is this?" said Electra. "Speakest thou of trouble greater than that which I now endure?"

"Surely," the other made reply, "for they will send thee far hence, and shut thee up where thou shalt never more see the light of the sun, if thou stayest not these complaints."

But Electra did not fear one whit to hear these things, but waxed fiercer in her anger. And, after a while, as the strife ceased not between them, Chrysothemis would have gone on her way. And when Electra perceived this, she asked her for what purpose and whither she was carrying these offerings to the dead.

And Chrysothemis made reply that she was carrying them at the bidding of her mother to the tomb of King Agamemnon. For that the Queen was in much fear, having seen a vision in the night which had sorely troubled her; and that the vision was this. The King her husband, whom she slew, seemed to bear her company, even as he had done in time past. And he took the sceptre which he had been wont to carry, and which Ægisthus carried after him, and planted it in the earth; and there sprang from it a very flourishing branch, by which the whole land of Mycenæ was overshadowed. "So much," she said, "I heard her say, when she told her dream to the light of the day; but more I know not, save that she sendeth me to make these offerings, by reason of her fear."

Then Electra answered, "Nay, my sister; lay not aught of these things upon our father's tomb, for they would be an abomination to him; but scatter them to the winds, or cover them with earth. So let them be kept for her, when she shall die. And surely, but that she is the most shameless of women, she had not sought to pay this honour to him whom she slew so foully. Thinketh she to atone in such sort for the blood that she hath shed? Not so. Put these things away; but thou and I will lay upon this tomb hair from thy head and from mine; small gifts, in truth, yet what we have. And do thou pray to our father that he will help us even where he dwelleth below the earth, and also that Orestes may come speedily, and set his foot upon the necks of them that hate us."

This Chrysothemis promised that she would do, and so departed. And in a short space came forth the Queen Clytæmnestra, and, finding her daughter Electra without the gate of the palace, was very wroth, saying that King Ægisthus had forbidden her to do this thing, and that it was not well that, he being absent, she should take no account of her mother.

"But now," she said, "let us reason together. Thou speakest ill of me, because I slew thy father. 'Tis even so. I deny it not. But mark, Justice slew him, not I only; and thou shouldest be on the side of Justice. He slew thy sister, sacrificing her to the Gods, as no other Greek had done. For what cause did he slay her? 'For the sake of the Greeks,' thou wilt say. But what had the Greeks to do with child of mine? Or was it for the sake of King Menelaüs his brother? But had not Menelaüs two children, and should not one of these have the rather died, seeing of what father and mother they came, even of those for whose sake the Greeks waged this war? Had Death, thinkest thou, desire for my children rather than for his? Or had this accursed father no care for my children, but only for the children of his brother? Surely this was the deed of a foolish and wicked man. Aye, I say it, whatever thou mayest think, and so would say she who died, could she take voice and speak."

Then said Electra, "If thou permittest, I would say somewhat for him and for her."

And the Queen answered, "Say on. Didst thou always speak in such mood, thou wert not so ill to hear."

Then Electra spake: "Thou sayest, 'I slew thy father.' 'Tis enough. Worse thou couldst not say, whether 'twere justly done or no. But of justice thou hadst never a thought. 'Twas the ill persuasion of him with whom thou now consortest that urged thee to this deed. And as for my sister, thou knowest well that my father slew a stag in the grove of Artemis, and boasted himself of the deed, and that the goddess was wroth with him, and hindered the voyage of the Greeks; and that for this cause my father slew his daughter, knowing that otherwise the ships could sail neither to Troy nor homewards. Yea, he slew her, sorely against his will, for the people's sake, and for nought else. But consider whether this that thou sayest be not altogether a pretence. Art thou not wife to him that was thy fellow in this deed? Callest thou this taking vengeance for thy daughter that was slain? And thy children—art thou a mother to them? What ill do not I suffer at thy hand and the hand of thy partner? And Orestes, whom I barely saved from thy hand, liveth he not in exile? Surely, whatsoever it be that thou chargest against him, thou hast no cause to be ashamed of me."

Then the two spake many bitter words to each other; and at the last, when Electra held her peace, the Queen prayed to the Gods, and made her offerings to the tomb. And first she addressed herself to Phœbus: "O Phœbus, hear that which is in my heart; for to say the thing aloud I dare not, seeing that I am not among friends. But of the dreams that I saw this night past, grant that the good be accomplished and the evil be turned away to my enemies; and that I be not cast down from the wealth wherein I now live; and that I may wield this sceptre of the son of Atreus which now I have, and may have the company of my friends, even as now, and the love of my children, if so be that they love their mother."

And while she thus spake, the old man came in, and would fain know whether that which he saw was the palace of Atreus. And when he heard that it was, he asked whether the lady whom he saw was the Queen. And hearing this also, he spake, "Lady, I have good tidings for thee and King Ægisthus."

"First tell me who thou art."

"I come from Phanoteus of Phocis: I bring great news."

"Tell me; for the man is a friend, and the tidings, I doubt not, good."

"I will say it in one word—Orestes is dead."

And when Electra heard this, she brake forth into a great cry, saying that she was undone. But the Queen said, "What? What sayest thou? Heed not this woman."

And the man said, "I told thee, and tell thee yet again, that Orestes is dead."

And again Electra brake forth into a cry; but the Queen bade her hold her peace, and would have the stranger tell the story. And the man said—

"He came to Delphi, whither the Greeks greatly resort, purposing to contend in the games of the Pythian Apollo. And first there was a race of runners on foot; and for this he came forward, and passing all that ran with him so won the prize. Nor indeed did I ever see such a man; for there was not one contest in which he had not the pre-eminence. Very fair was he to look upon, and his name, he said, was Orestes of Argos, and he was the son of that Agamemnon who in days past was captain of the host of the Greeks at Troy. But when the Gods are minded to destroy a man, who is so strong that he can escape? It fell out then that on the next day at sunset there was proclaimed a race of chariots, to which there came one man from Achaia, and from Sparta one, and two from Barca in Africa. After these came Orestes, being the fifth, with horses of Thessaly. And the sixth was a man of Ætolia, with bay horses, and the seventh a man of Magnesia in Thessaly, and the eighth was a man of Œnea, whose horses were white, and the ninth from Athens, a city which, they say, was builded of Gods, and a Bœotian was the tenth. First the heralds shook lots for each in a helmet, and each man had his place according as his lot came forth. And after this the trumpet sounded, and the horses leapt forward, while the men shouted to them and shook the reins, and spared not the goad. Great was the noise, and the dust rose up like a cloud from the plain. And on the backs of the charioteers and on the wheels of them that went before came the foam from the horses that followed, so close did they lie together. And Orestes, when he came to the pillar where the chariots turned, drave so that his wheel wellnigh touched it, and slackened the rein for the right horse, and pressed on that which was on the left. So far no mishap had befallen the chariots, but all had fared well. But here the steeds of the man of Œnea, being very hard to hold, brake from their course, and drave against the side of one of the chariots from Barca. And now they had ended six courses, and were about to begin the seventh. But with this beginning of trouble went all things wrong, for one drave against another till all the plain of Crissa was covered with broken chariots as the sea with shipwrecks. But the man of Athens was very skilful in driving, and, when he saw the beginning of confusion, he drew his horses aside and held back, and so escaped without damage. Now Orestes was the hindermost of all, trusting to what he should do at the end; and when he saw that only the man of Athens was left, he shouted to his horses and made haste to come up with him. Then the two drave together, having their chariots equal, and first one showed somewhat in the front and then the other. And for eleven courses of the twelve all went well with Orestes; but as he was rounding the pillar for the last time, he loosed the left rein and knew not that he loosed it overmuch, and smote against the pillar and brake his axle in the midst, and so was thrown out of his chariot; but the reins were tangled about him and held him. And all the people cried aloud when they saw the young man dragged over the plain. But at last they that had driven the other chariots hardly stayed the horses, and loosed him. Covered with blood was he and sorely mangled, that none could have known him. And we burnt his body; and certain Phocians, whom the Prince hath sent for this purpose, bring that which remaineth of him, being but a few ashes in an urn of brass, for all he was so tall and strong. This is a sad tale for thee to hear; but for us who saw it never was anything in this world more grievous."

Then the Queen said, "Shall I say that this hath happened ill or well? or that it is an evil thing, yet profitable to me? Surely it is grievous that I find safety in the death of my own kindred."

"What troubleth thee, lady, in these news?" said the false messenger.

"'Tis a dreadful thing to be a mother. Whatever wrong she suffereth she cannot hurt him whom she bare."

"Then," said he, "it seemeth that I have come in vain."

"Not so," the Queen made answer, "if thou showest proof that Orestes is dead. For he hath long been a stranger to me, and when he departed hence he knew me not, being very young; and of late, accusing me of the blood of his father, he hath made dreadful threats against me, so that I could not sleep in peace day or night. And now this day I am quit of this fear that wasted my very life."

Then the Queen and the false messenger went into the palace; and when they were gone Electra cried, saying, "See here, forsooth, a mother that weepeth and mourneth for her son! O my Orestes, how utterly hast thou undone me! For now all the hope I had is gone that thou wouldst come and avenge my father. Whither can I go, for thou and he are gone? Must I be as a slave among them that slew my father? This gate at least I will enter no more. If I weary them, let them slay me, if they will; I should count it a grace so to die."

And the maidens of Argos bewailed the dead brother with her. But in the midst of their lamentations came Chrysothemis in great joy, saying, "O my sister, I bring thee good tidings that will give thee ease from thy sorrows!"

"What ease, when they are past all remedy?"

"Orestes is here. Know this as surely as thou now seest me before thee."

"Surely thou art mad, and laughest at thy woes and mine."

"Not so. By the hearth of my fathers I swear it. Orestes is here."

"Who told thee this tale that thou believest so strangely?"

"'Tis from proofs that I saw with mine own eyes, and not another's, that I believe. Listen, therefore. When I came to the tomb of my father, I saw on the top of the pillar offerings of milk that had been newly poured, and garlands of all manner of flowers. And marvelling much at this, I looked to see if any man was at hand; and seeing none, I drew near; and on the tomb I espied a lock of hair newly cut; and as soon as I espied it I knew that it was a token of Orestes, dearest of men in all the world to thee and me. And as I touched it I held my tongue from all words that might do hurt, and my eyes were filled with tears. And now think whose should this be but his? Who should do this but thou or I; and I did not, nor thou, who canst not go so far from this house; and my mother is not wont to do such things. 'Tis Orestes surely. And now sorrow hath passed away, and all things will be well."

"Nay," Electra made answer, "I pity thee for thy folly.'

"Do not my tidings please thee?"

"I know not why thou talkest so wildly."

"But may I not believe that which I have seen with mine own eyes?"

"O my sister, he is dead! Look not to him for help any more."

"But stay. From whom didst thou learn this?"

"From one who was at hand when he perished."

"Where is he? This is passing strange. Whose then could be these offerings on the tomb?"

"Some one hath put them for a remembrance of the dead Orestes."

"Woe is me, and I made haste with the good tidings, as I thought, and knew not what new trouble worse than the old had fallen upon us."

Then said Electra, "Hear now what I purpose. Thou knowest that we are utterly bereaved of friends, for Death hath devoured them all. Now, while Orestes yet lived and was prosperous, I hoped that he would come to avenge our father's death. But now that he is dead, I look to thee, that thou shouldest make common cause with me and work this vengeance on them that slew him. Canst thou endure that we should live deprived of the wealth that was our father's; and also that we should grow old unmated? For know that a husband thou shalt never have, for indeed Ægisthus is not unwise that he should suffer children to be born of thee or me to be a manifest damage to himself. But if thou wilt hearken to me, first thou wilt do that which is fitting to thy father and brother that are dead; and next thou wilt win great renown, and be married to a noble mate, for all men are wont to regard that which is worthy. And surely in days to come some man, citizen or stranger, that seeth us will say, ' Look, my friends, at these sisters, for they wrought deliverance for the house of their father, and spared not their own lives, but slew their enemies in the day of their prosperity. These must we love and reverence; these on feast days, and when the city is gathered together, must we honour by reason of their courage.' Wherefore, my sister, be of good heart. Be bold for thy father's sake and for thy brother's, for mine also and for thine, that we may be delivered from these troubles. For to them of noble breeding to live basely is a shame."

But Chrysothemis made answer, "O my sister, how didst thou find such daring purpose as this, making ready thyself as for fight, and calling me to follow? Knowest thou not that thou art a woman and no man, and that thou art weaker than thine enemies, and that their good luck ever increaseth and ours groweth less and less? And what will it profit us if we get great renown, yet die in shameful fashion? And yet to die I think not such loss, but to wish to die and not attain to it, suffering torture or bonds. Keep thy anger within bounds. What thou hast said I will count as unsaid. Only yield to them that are stronger."

And after many words, Electra urging her sister to this deed and the other excusing herself, the two parted in great anger. And Chrysothemis went into the palace, but Electra abode where she was. And to her, after a while, came Orestes, but disguised that no man might know him, and asked the Argive maidens that stood by, whether the house that he beheld was the palace of King Ægisthus, and when he heard that it was so, he bade them tell the King that certain Phocian strangers were come seeking him. But when Electra heard it, she said, "Comest thou with proof of this ill news that we have heard?"

And Orestes made answer, "I know not what news thou speakest of, but the old man, Strophius, the Phocian, bade me bring tidings of Orestes."

"What are thy tidings, though I tremble to hear them?"

"We are come bringing all that remaineth of him in this urn."

And when Electra saw it she cried that they should give the urn into her hands; and Orestes bade them do so. And she took it and said, "O Orestes, that wast dearer to me than all men else, how different is this coming of thine to that which I had hoped! Lovely wert thou when I sent thee from this house, and now I hold thee in my hands and thou art naught. Would to the Gods thou hadst died that day when thy father was slain; for now thou art dead, an exile, and in the land of strangers, and I paid thee no office of kindness nor took thy ashes from the funeral fire; but this did strangers for thee, and now thou comest a handful of ashes in a little urn. Woe is me for the wasted pains of nurture and the toil wherewith out of a willing heart I tended thee! For thy mother loved thee not more than I, nor was any one but I thy nurse. And now all this hath departed. My father is dead, and thou art dead, and my enemies laugh me to scorn, and thy mother that is no mother is mad with joy. Let me die with thee, for 'tis the dead alone whom I see to be quit of pain."

But while she so spake Orestes was much troubled in heart and knew not what to do. But at the last he said, "Is this the Princess Electra whom I see?"

And she answered, "Even so, and very ill she fareth."

Then he looked upon her again and said to himself, "What a noble lady is this, and in what ungodly fashion hath she been afflicted!"

And when Electra would know why he was so troubled, he said, "It paineth me to see thee excelling all women in sorrow."

"Nay," she said, "thou seest but a small part of my sorrows."

"Hast thou, then, yet worse to bear than these?"

"Yea, for I live with them that are murderers."

"Whom sayest thou they murdered?"

"They murdered my father—and I am constrained to serve them."

"Who constraineth thee?"

"A mother that is no mother."

"And is there none that can help thee?"

"None, for him that was my helper thou bringest in this urn. But why pitiest thou me as doth no other man? Art thou, perchance, a kinsman?"

"Put down this urn and I will tell thee."

"Nay, stranger, take this not from me, for it holds all that is dearest to me."

"Speak not such idle words: thy sorrow is without cause."

"Sayest thou 'without cause' when my brother is dead?"

"Thou dost ill to speak thus of thy brother."

"Doth the dead then think so lightly of me?"

"No man thinketh lightly of thee; yet with these ashes thou hast no concern."

"How so, if this is the body of my Orestes?"

"Here is no true body, only one that is feigned."

"Unhappy man! where, then, is his tomb?"

"He hath none—what need hath the living of a tomb?"

"Liveth he, then?"

"Yea, if I am alive."

"Art thou, then, he?"

"Yea; look at this my father's seal, and say whether I speak truly."

And when she saw the seal, she knew that it was her father's, and that this stranger was indeed Orestes. And she cried aloud for joy, and embraced him. Then, after the two had talked together for a very brief space, Orestes said, "Tell me not how ill thy mother hath done, nor how Ægisthus hath wasted the substance of my house; but rather instruct me in this: shall I do this thing secretly or openly? Take heed also lest thy mother see thee bear a joyful face, and so take warning."

And Electra made answer, "As for this present, know that Ægisthus is absent, and that the Queen is alone. Therefore do as thou deemest best. And as for me, be sure that I shall not cease from tears; for the old sorrow is inveterate in me; and also, now that I have seen thee, I weep for joy."

But while they talked together came the old man in haste, and rebuked them that they so spent the time; and to Orestes he said that no one knew him who he was, but that all deemed him dead, and that he must make haste and do the deed; for that now the Queen was alone, nor was there any man in the palace.

And Orestes, having prayed to the Gods, and especially to Apollo, who indeed had bidden him do this work, went into the palace. And at the first Electra went with him, but afterwards hastened out, to keep watch, lest perchance King Ægisthus should return. So she and the woman waited without and listened. And after a while there came a cry, " O my son, my son, have pity on thy mother." And Electra said, " Aye, but thou hadst no pity on him, or on the father that begat him." And then again a cry, " Woe is me! I am smitten." And Electra said, " Smite, if thou canst, a double blow." And then the voice came a third time, " I am smitten again." But Electra made reply, " Would that Ægisthus were smitten with thee!" After this Orestes came forth, with his sword dripping with blood. And when the women asked him how it fared in the palace, he answered, "All is well, if only Apollo hath spoken the thing that is true."

But as he spake King Ægisthus came back, asking, "Where be these strangers from Phocis that are come, telling how Prince Orestes hath come by his death in a chariot race?"

And Electra made answer that they were within. Then Ægisthus cried, "Open the gates, and let all men of Argos and of Mycenæ see the body; and if perchance any man hath been lifted up with vain hopes, let him look upon Orestes that he is dead, and so submit himself to me."

Then the gate was opened, and there appeared a dead body, lying covered with a sheet. And Ægisthus said, "Take the covering from off his face; for he is my kinsman, and should not miss due mourning from me."

But Orestes answered, "Take it thyself; for this dead body is thine, not mine."

Then said Ægisthus, "Thou speakest well: if the Queen be within the palace, bid her come."

And Orestes said, " She is near thee ; look not elsewhere." And when Ægisthus lifted the covering, lo ! it was the Queen who lay dead. Then he knew the whole matter, and turned to the stranger saying, " Thou must be Orestes."

" 'Tis even so," cried Orestes. " And now go into the palace."

" But why slayest thou me in darkness, if this deed be just ? "

" I slay thee where thou didst slay him that is dead."

So he drave him before him into the palace, and slew him there. Thus the blood of King Agamemnon was avenged.

THE STORY OF THE FURIES, OR THE LOOSING OF ORESTES.

The gift of prophecy Earth had at the first, and after her Themis; and after her Phœbe, who was of the race of the Titans, and Phœbe gave it to Apollo—who is also called Phœbus—at his birth. Now Apollo had a great temple and famous upon the hill of Delphi, to which men were wont to resort from all the earth, seeking counsel and knowledge of the things that should come to pass hereafter. And it came to pass on a day that the priestess—for the temple was served by a woman, whom men called Pythia—when she went into the shrine, after her custom, in the morning, saw therein a dreadful sight. For by the very seat of the God there sat a man, a suppliant, whose hands were dripping with blood, and he bare a bloody sword, and on his head there was a garland of olive leaves, cunningly twined with snow-white wool. And behind there sat a strange company of women sleeping, if indeed they could be called women, that were more hideous than the Gorgons, on which if a man looks he is turned to stone, or the Harpies, of which they say that they have the faces of women and the bodies of vultures. Now this man was Orestes, and the blood that was upon his hands was the blood of his mother Clytæmnestra, whom he slew, taking vengeance for his father King Agamemnon, and the women were the Furies, who pursue them that shed the blood of kindred, and torment them even unto death. But the priestess when she saw this sight fell down for fear and crawled forth from the temple. And when she was gone there appeared Apollo himself. Now Apollo had counselled Orestes that he should slay his mother, and so avenge his father's blood that had been shed. And now he spake, saying, " Fear not, I will not betray thee, but will keep to thee to the end. But now thou must flee from this place ; and know that these, the hateful ones, with whom neither God nor man nor beast consorts, will pursue thee both over the sea and over the land; but do thou not grow weary or faint, but haste to the city of Pallas, and sit in the temple of the goddess, throwing thy arms about the image, and there will I contrive that which shall loose thee from this guilt."

And when the God had said this, he bade his brother Hermes (for he also stood near) to guide the man by the way in which he should go.

So Orestes went his way. And straightway, when he was gone, rose up the spirit of Queen Clytæmnestra, clad in garments of black, and on her neck was the wound where her son smote her. And the spirit spake to the Furies, for these were yet fast asleep, saying, "Sleep ye? What profit is there in them that sleep? Shamefully do ye dishonour me among the dead; for they whom I slew reproach me, and my cause, though I was slain by my own son, no one taketh in hand. Do ye not mind with what sufferings, with what midnight sacrifices upon the hearth in old time I honoured you, and now, while ye sleep, this wretch hath escaped from the net."

Then they began to stir and rouse them-

THE LOOSING OF ORESTES. 189

selves, the spirit still goading them with angry words till they were now fully awake and ready to pursue. Then there appeared the God Apollo with his silver bow in his hand, and cried, " Depart from this place, ye accursed ones. Depart with all speed, lest an arrow leap forth from this string and smite you so that ye vomit forth the blood of men that ye have drunk. This is no fit halting-place for you; in the habitations of cruelty is your best abode, or in some lion's den, dripping with blood, not, verily, where men come to hear the oracles of truth. Depart ye, therefore, with all speed."

" Nay," said they; " hear, King Apollo, what we would say. For thou art verily guilty of this matter."

" How so? So much thou mayest say."

"Thou badest this stranger slay his mother."

" I bade him take vengeance for his father's blood."

" And thou wast ready to answer for this deed?"

" I bade him come for succour to this shrine."

" Yet they who attend him please thee not?"

"No, for it fitteth not that they should approach this place."

"Yet 'tis our appointed task to follow him that slayeth his mother."

"And what if a wife slay her husband?"

"Between wife and husband there is no kindred blood."

"Thou dost dishonour, saying this, to great Heré that is wife to Zeus, and to all love, than which there is nothing dearer to men."

"Yet will I hunt this man to the death, for the blood of his mother drives me on."

"And I will help him and save him."

But in the meantime Orestes fled with all speed to the city of Athens, and came to the temple of Athené, and sat clasping the image of the goddess, and cried to her that he was come at the bidding of Apollo, and was ready to abide her judgment. But the Furies followed hard upon him, having tracked him as a dog tracks a fawn that hath been wounded, by the blood. And when they were come and had found him in the temple, they cried that it was of no avail that he sought the help of the Gods, for that the blood of his mother that had been shed cried against him from the ground, and that they would drink his blood, and waste him, and drive him a living man among the dead, that all men might shun to do such deeds in time to come.

Then said Orestes, " I have learnt in many troubles both how to be silent and how to speak. And now I speak as a wise man biddeth me. For lo! the stain of blood that is upon my hand groweth pale, and the defilement is cleansed away. Therefore, I call to Athené that is Queen of this land, to help me, wherever she be; for though she be far, yet being a goddess, she can hear my voice. And helping me, she shall gain me, and my people, and my land to be friends to her and to her people for ever."

But not the less did the Furies cry out against him that he was accursed and given over to them as a prey; for that they were appointed of the Gods to execute vengeance upon evil-doers, of whom he was the chief, seeing that he had slain the mother that bare him.

But while they thus cried out against him, there appeared the Goddess Athené, very fair to see, with the spear of gold in her hand; and she spake, saying, "From the banks of Scamander am I come, for I heard the cry of one that called upon my name. And now I would fain know what meaneth all this that I see. Who art thou, stranger, that sittest clasping this image? And who are ye that are so strange of aspect, being like neither to the Gods nor to the daughters of men?"

Then the Furies made answer, "We will tell thee the matter shortly, daughter of Zeus. We are the children of Night, and we are called the Curses, and our office is to drive the murderer from his home."

Then said the goddess, "And whither do ye drive him?"

"We drive him to the land where no joy abideth."

"And why do ye pursue this man?"

"Because he dared to slay his mother."

"Did aught compel him to this deed?"

"What should compel a man to such wickedness?"

"There are two stories to be told, and I have heard but one."

And when they had thus talked together for

a while the Furies said that they would abide by the judgment of the goddess. Whereupon she turned herself to Orestes, and bade him set forth his case; who he was, and what deed he had done. To which he made this answer: "I am a man of Argos, and my sire, King Agamemnon, thou knowest well; for he was ruler of the host of the Greeks, and by his hands thou madest the great city of Troy to be no city. Now this man perished in a most unrighteous fashion, when he was returned to his home, for my mother, having an evil heart, slew him foully in the bath. And I, coming back to my country, from which in time past I had fled, slew her that bare me. This I deny not. Yea, I slew her, taking vengeance for my father. And in this matter Apollo hath a common share with me, for he said that great woes should pierce my heart if I recompensed not them that had done this deed. But do thou judge this matter; for with thy judgment, whatsoever it be, I will be content."

Then the goddess said, "This is a hard matter to judge; for thou, Orestes, art come as a suppliant to this house, being innocent of guilt, and I may not reject thee. And yet these have a suit which may not lightly be dismissed; for haply, if they fail of that which they seek, they will send a wasting disease upon this land and consume it. But seeing that this great matter has fallen to me to deal with, I will do this. Judges will I choose, binding them with an oath, and they shall judge in all cases, whensoever one man hath slain another. And this will I stablish for all time to come. Do you, therefore, call witnesses and proofs with oaths for confirmation thereof. And I will choose such as are worthiest among my citizens, righteous men, who will have regard unto their oath, and they shall judge this matter."

So they went all of them to the hill of Ares, where the cause should be judged. And twelve men that were worthiest in the city sat on the seat of judgment, and Athené came forth and said to the herald that stood by, "Blow the trumpet, that the people keep silence, and that this cause may be tried justly, as is meet."

Then came forth Apollo. And when tne Furies saw him they cried, "What hast thou to do with this matter, King Apollo?"

And he said, "As a witness am I come, for I commanded this man to do this deed."

Then Athené commanded that the Furies should speak the first, being the accusers. So they began saying to Orestes, "Answer what we shall ask thee. Didst thou slay thy mother?"

"I slew her. This I deny not."

"How didst thou slay her?"

"I drew my sword, and smote her on the neck."

"Who counselled thee to this deed?"

"Apollo counselled me; therefore I fear not; also my father shall help me from the tomb."

"Shall the dead help thee that didst slay thy mother?"

"Yea, for she also had slain her husband. Say, why did ye not pursue her while she lived?"

"Because she was not akin to him she slew."

"Not akin? then was I not akin to her. But do thou bear witness, King Apollo."

Then said Apollo, "I am a prophet and lie not. Never have I spoken about man or woman or city save as my Father Zeus gave me to speak."

Then said the Furies, "How sayest thou?

that Zéus gave this command that this man should slay his mother?"

" 'Twas even so. For think how basely this woman slew her husband, his father. For she smote him not with an arrow, as might some Amazon, but when he was come back from the war, full of honour, in the bath she entangled him, wrapping a robe about him, and so slew him. Wherefore this man did righteously, taking vengeance for the blood that was shed. And as for this kinship that ye say is between a man and his mother, hearken to this. Had Pallas here a mother? Nay, for no womb bare her, seeing that she came from the head of Zeus her father."

Then said Athené, "It is enough. Judges, judge ye this cause, doing justice therein. But first hear the statute that I make establishing this court. On this hill did the Amazons in old time build their fortress when they waged war with King Theseus and the men of this land; and hence it is called the hill of Ares, who is the god of war. And here do I make this as an ordinance for ever, that it may be a bulwark to this land; that judges may sit herein, keen to avenge the wrong, not blinding their eyes

THE LOOSING OF ORESTES. 197

with gifts, but doing true judgment and justice between man and man. And now rise, ye judges, from your place, and take these pebbles in your hand, and vote according to right, not forgetting your oath."

So the judges rose up from their place and dropped the pebbles into the urns, Apollo on the one side and the Furies on the other urging them with many promises and threats. And at the last Athené stood up and said, "'Tis for me to give the casting vote; and I give it to Orestes. For I myself was not born of a mother; wherefore I am on the father's side. And I care not to avenge the death of a woman that slew her husband, the ruler of her house. Now, if the votes be equal, Orestes is free. Take the pebbles from the urns, ye to whom this office is given. And see that ye do it justly and well, that no wrong be done."

So they that were appointed to this took the pebbles forth from the urns and counted them. And lo! the votes were equal on this side and on that. And Athené stood forth and said, " The man is free."

Thus was accomplished the loosing of Orestes.

THE STORY OF IPHIGENIA AMONG THE TAURIANS.

It has been told in the story of King Agamemnon that the Goddess Artemis, being wroth with him because he had slain a hart which she loved, suffered not the ships of the Greeks to sail till he had offered his daughter Iphigenia for a sacrifice. But when the King consented, and all things had been made ready for slaying the maiden, the goddess would not that her blood should be shed, but put a fair hind in her place, and carried away the maiden to the land of the Taurians, where she had a temple and an altar. Now on this altar the King of the land was wont to sacrifice any stranger, being Greek by nation, who was driven by stress of weather to the place, for none went thither willingly. And the name of the King was Thoas, which signifieth in the Greek tongue, "swift of foot."

Now when the maiden had been there many years she dreamed a dream. And in the dream she seemed to have departed from the land of the Taurians and to dwell in the city of Argos, wherein she had been born. And as she slept in the women's chamber there befell a great earthquake, and cast to the ground the palace of her fathers, so that there was left one pillar only which stood upright. And as she looked on this pillar, yellow hair seemed to grow upon it as the hair of a man, and it spake with a man's voice. And she did to it as she was wont to do to the strangers that were sacrificed upon the altar, purifying it with water, and weeping the while. And the interpretation of the dream she judged to be that her brother Orestes was dead, for that male children are the pillars of a house, and that he only was left to the house of her father.

Now it chanced that at this same time Orestes, with Pylades that was his friend, came in a ship to the land of the Taurians. And the cause of his coming was this. After that he had slain his mother, taking vengeance for the death of King Agamemnon his father, the Furies pursued him. Then Apollo, who had commanded him to do this deed, bade him go to the land of Athens that he might be judged. And when he had been judged and loosed, yet the Furies left him not. Wherefore Apollo commanded that he should sail for the land of the Taurians and carry there the image of Artemis and bring it to the land of the Athenians, and that after this he should have rest. Now when the two were come to the place, they saw the altar that it was red with the blood of them that had been slain thereon. And Orestes doubted how they might accomplish the things for the which he was come, for the walls of the temple were high, and the gates not easy to be broken through. Therefore he would have fled to the ship, but Pylades consented not, seeing that they were not wont to go back from that to which they had set their hand, but counselled that they should hide themselves during the day in a cave that was hard by the seashore, not near to the ship, lest search should be made for them, and that by night they should creep into the temple by a space that there was between the pillars, and carry off the image, and so depart.

So they hid themselves in a cavern by the sea. But it chanced that certain herdsmen were feeding their oxen in pastures hard by the shore; one of these, coming near to the cavern, spied the young men as they sat therein, and stealing back to his fellows, said, "See ye not them that sit yonder. Surely they are Gods;" for they were exceeding tall and fair to look upon. And some began to pray to them, thinking that they might be the Twin Brethren or of the sons of Nereus. But another laughed and said, "Not so; these are shipwrecked men who hide themselves, knowing that it is our custom to sacrifice strangers to our Gods." To him the others gave consent, and said that they should take the men prisoners that they might be sacrificed to the Gods.

But while they delayed Orestes ran forth from the cave, for the madness was come upon him, crying out, "Pylades, seest thou not that dragon from hell; and that who would kill me with the serpents of her mouth, and this again that breatheth out fire, holding my mother in her arms to cast her upon me?" And first he bellowed as a bull and then howled as a dog, for the Furies, he said, did so. But the herdsmen, when they saw this, gathered together in great fear and sat down. But when Orestes drew his sword and leapt, as a lion might leap, into the midst of the herd, slaying the beasts (for he thought in his madness that he was contending with the Furies), then the herdsmen, blowing on shells, called to the people of the land; for they feared the young men, so strong they seemed and valiant. And when no small number was gathered together, they began to cast stones and javelins at the two. And now the madness of Orestes began to abate, and Pylades tended him carefully, wiping away the foam from his mouth, and holding his garments before him that he should not be wounded by the stones. But when Orestes came to himself, and beheld in what straits they were, he groaned aloud and cried, "We must die, O Pylades, only let us die as befitteth brave men. Draw thy sword and follow me." And the people of the land dared not to stand before them; yet while some fled, others would cast stones at them. For all that no man wounded them. But at the last, coming about them with a great multitude, they smote the swords out of their hands with stones, and so bound them and took them to King Thoas. And the King commanded that they should be taken to the temple, that the priestess might deal with them according to the custom of the place.

So they brought the young men bound to the temple. Now the name of the one they knew, for they had heard his companion call to him, but the name of the other they knew not. And when Iphigenia saw them, she bade the people loose their bonds, for that being holy to the goddess they were free. And then —for she took the two for brothers—she asked them, saying, " Who is your mother, and your father, and your sister, if a sister you have ? She will be bereaved of noble brothers this day. And whence come ye ? "

To her Orestes answered, " What meanest thou, lady, by lamenting in this fashion over us ? I hold it folly in him who must die that he should bemoan himself. Pity us not; we know what manner of sacrifices ye have in this land."

"Tell me now, which of ye two is called Pylades?"

"Not I, but this my companion."

"Of what city in the land of Greece are ye? And are ye brothers born of one mother?"

"Brothers we are, but in friendship, not in blood."

"And what is thy name?"

"That I tell thee not. Thou hast power over my body, but not over my name."

"Wilt thou not tell me thy country?"

And when he told her that his country was Argos, she asked him many things, as about Troy, and Helen, and Calchas the prophet, and Ulysses; and at last she said, "And Achilles, son of Thetis of the sea, is he yet alive?"

"He is dead, and his marriage that was made at Aulis is of no effect."

"A false marriage it was, as some know full well."

"Who art thou that inquirest thus about matters in Greece?"

"I am of the land of Greece, and was

brought thence yet being a child. But there was a certain Agamemnon, son of Atreus, what of him?"

"I know not. Lady, leave all talk of him."

"Say not so; but do me a pleasure, and tell me."

"He is dead."

"Woe is me! How died he?"

"What meaneth thy sorrow? Art thou of his kindred?"

"'Tis a pity to think how great he was, and now he hath perished."

"He was slain in a most miserable fashion by a woman. But ask no more."

"Only this one thing. Is his wife yet alive?"

"Nay; for the son whom she bare slew her, taking vengeance for his father."

"A dreadful deed, but righteous withal."

"Righteous indeed he is, but the Gods love him not."

"And did the King leave any other child behind him?"

"One daughter, Electra by name."

"And is his son yet alive?"

"He is alive, but no man more miserable."

Now when Iphigenia heard that he was alive, and knew that she had been deceived by the dreams which she had dreamt, she conceived a thought in her heart, and said to Orestes, "Hearken now, for I have somewhat to say to thee that shall bring profit both to thee and to me. Wilt thou, if I save thee from this death, carry tidings of me to Argos to my friends, and bear a tablet from me to them? For such a tablet I have with me, which one who was brought captive to this place wrote for me, pitying me, for he knew that I caused not his death, but the law of the goddess in this place. Nor have I yet found a man who should carry this thing to Argos. But thou, I judge, art of noble birth, and knowest the city and those with whom I would have communication. Take then this tablet, and thy life as a reward; and let this man be sacrificed to the goddess."

Then Orestes made answer, "Thou hast said well, lady, save in one thing only. That this man should be sacrificed in my stead pleaseth me not at all. For I am he that brought this voyage to pass; and this man came with me that he might help me in my troubles. Wherefore it would be a grievous wrong that he should suffer in my stead and I escape. Give then the tablet to him. He shall take it to the city of Argos, and thou shalt have what thou wilt. But as for me, let them slay me, if they will."

"'Tis well spoken, young man. Thou art come, I know, of a noble stock. The Gods grant that my brother—for I have a brother, though he be far hence—may be such as thou. It shall be as thou wilt. This man shall depart with the tablet, and thou shalt die."

Then Orestes would know the manner of the death by which he must die. And she told him that she slew not the victims with her own hand, but that there were ministers in the temple appointed to this office, she preparing them for sacrifice beforehand. Also she said that his body would be burned with fire.

And when Orestes had wished that the hand of his sister might pay due honour to him in his death, she said, "This may not be, for she is far away from this strange land. But yet, seeing that thou art a man of Argos, I myself will adorn thy tomb, and pour oil of olives and honey on thy ashes." Then she departed, that she might fetch the tablet from her dwelling, bidding the attendants keep the young men fast, but without bonds.

But when she was gone, Orestes said to Pylades, "Pylades, what thinkest thou? Who is this maiden? She had great knowledge of things in Troy and Argos, and of Calchas the wise soothsayer, and of Achilles and the rest. And she made lamentation over King Agamemnon. She must be of Argos."

And Pylades answered, "This I cannot say; all men have knowledge of what befell the King. But hearken to this. It were shame to me to live if thou diest. I sailed with thee, and will die with thee. For otherwise men will account lightly of me both in Argos and in Phocis, which is my own land, thinking that I betrayed thee, or basely slew thee, that I might have thy kingdom, marrying thy sister, who shall inherit it in thy stead. Not so: I will die with thee, and my body shall be burnt together with thine."

But Orestes answered, "I must bear my own troubles. This indeed would be a shameful thing, that when thou seekest to help me, I should destroy thee. But as for me, seeing how the Gods deal with me, it is well that I should die. Thou, indeed, art happy, and thy house is blessed; but my house is accursed. Go, therefore, and my sister, whom I have given thee to wife, shall bear thee children, and the house of my father shall not perish. And I charge thee that when thou art safe returned to the city of Argos, thou do these things. First, thou shalt build a tomb for me, and my sister shall make an offering there of her hair and of her tears also. And tell her that I died, slain by a woman of Argos, that offered me as an offering to her Gods; and I charge thee that thou leave not my sister, but be faithful to her. And now farewell, true friend and companion in my toils; for indeed I die, and Phœbus hath lied unto me, prophesying falsely."

And Pylades sware to him that he would build him a tomb, and be a true husband to his sister. After this Iphigenia came forth, holding a tablet in her hand. And she said, "Here is the tablet of which I spake. But I fear lest he to whom I shall give it shall haply take no account of it when he is returned to the land. Therefore I would fain bind him with an oath that he will deliver it to them that should have it in the city of Argos." And Orestes consented, saying that she also should bind herself with an oath that she would deliver one of the two from death. So she sware by Artemis that she would persuade the King, and deliver Pylades from death. And Pylades sware on his part by Zeus, the father of heaven, that he would give the tablet to those whom it should concern. And having sworn it, he said, "But what if a storm overtake me, and the tablet be lost, and I only be saved?"

"I will tell thee what hath been written in the tablet; and if it perish, thou shalt tell them again; but if not, then thou shalt give it as I bid thee."

"And to whom shall I give it?"

"Thou shalt give it to Orestes, son of Agamemnon. And that which is written therein is this: 'I THAT WAS SACRIFICED IN AULIS, EVEN IPHIGENIA, WHO AM ALIVE AND YET DEAD TO MY OWN PEOPLE, BID THEE——'"

But when Orestes heard this, he brake in,

"Where is this Iphigenia? Hath the dead come back among the living?"

"Thou seest her in me. But interrupt me not. 'I BID THEE FETCH ME BEFORE I DIE TO ARGOS FROM A STRANGE LAND, TAKING ME FROM THE ALTAR THAT IS RED WITH THE BLOOD OF STRANGERS, WHEREAT I SERVE.' And if Orestes ask by what means I am alive, thou shalt say that Artemis put a hind in my stead, and that the priest, thinking that he smote me with the knife, slew the beast, and that the goddess brought me to this land."

Then said Pylades, "My oath is easy to keep. Orestes, take thou this tablet from thy sister."

Then Orestes embraced his sister, crying—for she turned from him, not knowing what she should think—"O my sister, turn not from me; for I am thy brother whom thou didst not think to see."

And when she yet doubted, he told her of certain things by which she might know him to be Orestes—how that she had woven a tapestry wherein was set forth the strife between Atreus and Thyestes concerning the golden lamb; and that she had given a lock of her hair at Aulis to be a memorial of her; and that there was laid in her chamber at Argos the ancient spear of Pelops, her father's grandsire, with which he slew Œnomaüs, and won Hippodamia to be his wife.

And when she heard this, she knew that he was indeed Orestes, whom, being an infant and the latest born of his mother, she had in time past held in her arms. But when the two had talked together for a space, rejoicing over each other, and telling the things that had befallen them, Pylades said, "Greetings of friends after long parting are well; but we must needs consider how best we shall escape from this land of the barbarians."

But Iphigenia answered, "Yet nothing shall hinder me from knowing how fareth my sister Electra."

"She is married," said Orestes, "to this Pylades, whom thou seest."

"And of what country is he, and who is his father?"

"His father is Strophius the Phocian; and he is a kinsman, for his mother was the daughter of Atreus, and a friend also such as none other is to me."

Then Orestes set forth to his sister the cause of his coming to the land of the Taurians. And he said, "Now help me in this, my sister, that we may bear away the image of the goddess; for so doing I shall be quit of my madness, and thou wilt be brought to thy native country, and the house of thy father shall prosper. But if we do it not, then shall we perish altogether."

And Iphigenia doubted much how this thing might be done. But at the last she said, "I have a device whereby I shall compass the matter. I will say that thou art come hither, having murdered thy mother, and that thou canst not be offered for a sacrifice till thou art purified with the water of the sea. Also that thou hast touched the image, and that this also must be purified in like manner. And the image I myself will bear to the sea; for, indeed, I only may touch it with my hands. And of this Pylades also I will say that he is polluted in like manner with thee. So shall we three win our way to the ship. And that this be ready it will be thy care to provide."

And when she had so said, she prayed to Artemis: "Great goddess, that didst bring me safe in days past from Aulis, bring me now also, and these that are with me, safe to the land of Greece, so that men may count thy brother Apollo to be a true prophet. Nor shouldst thou be unwilling to depart from this barbarous land, and to dwell in the fair city of Athens."

After this came King Thoas, inquiring whether they had offered the strangers for sacrifice, and had duly burnt their bodies with fire. To him Iphigenia made answer, "These were unclean sacrifices that thou broughtest to me, O King."

"How didst thou learn this?"

"The image of the goddess turned upon her place of her own accord, and covered also her face with her hands."

"What wickedness, then, had these strangers wrought?"

"They slew their mother, and had been banished therefore from the land of Greece."

"O monstrous! Such deeds we barbarians never do. And now what dost thou purpose?"

"We must purify these strangers before we offer them for a sacrifice."

"With water from the river, or in the sea?"

"In the sea. The sea cleanseth away all that is evil among men."

"Well, thou hast it here, by the very walls of the temple."

"Aye, but I must seek a place apart from men."

"So be it; go where thou wilt; I would not look on things forbidden."

"The image also must be purified."

"Surely, if the pollution from these murderers of their mother hath touched it. This is well thought of in thee."

Then she instructed the King that he should bring the strangers out of the temple, having first bound them and veiled their heads. Also that certain of his guards should go with her, but that all the people of the city should be straitly commanded to stay within doors, that so they might not be defiled; and that he himself should abide in the temple, and purify it with fire, covering his head with his garments when the strangers should pass by.

"And be not troubled," she said, "if I seem to be long doing these things."

"Take what time thou wilt," he said "so that thou do all things in order."

So certain of the King's guards brought the two young men from out of the temple, and Iphigenia led them towards the place where the ship of Orestes lay at anchor. But when they were come near to the shore, she bade them halt nor come over near, for that she had that to do in which they must have no part. And she took the chain wherewith the young men were bound in her hands, and set up a strange song as of one that sought enchantments. And after that the guard sat where she bade them for a long time, they began to fear lest the strangers should have slain the priestess, and so fled. Yet they moved not, fearing to see that which was forbidden. But at the last with one consent they rose up. And when they were come to the sea, they saw the ship trimmed to set forth, and fifty sailors on the benches having oars in their hands ready for rowing ; and the two young men were standing unbound upon the shore near to the stern. And other sailors were dragging the ship by the cable to the shore that the young men might embark. Then the guards laid hold of the rudder, and sought to take it from his place, crying, "Who are ye that carry away priestesses and the images of our Gods?" Then Orestes said, "I am Orestes, and I carry away my sister." But the guards laid hold of Iphigenia; and when the sailors saw this they leapt from the ship; and neither the one nor the other had swords in their hands, but they fought with their fists and their feet also. And the sailors being strong and skilful, the King's men were driven back sorely bruised and wounded. And when they fled to a bank that was hard by and cast stones at the ship, the archers standing on the stern shot at them with arrows. Then—for his sister feared to come further—Orestes leapt into the sea, and raised her upon his shoulder and so lifted her into the ship, and the image of the goddess with her. And Pylades cried, "Lay hold of your oars, ye sailors, and smite the sea, for we have that for the which we came to this land." So the sailors rowed with all their might; and while the ship was in the harbour it went well with them, but when it was come to the open sea a great wave took it, for a violent wind blew against it, and drave it backwards to the shore.

And one of the guards when he saw this ran to King Thoas and told him, and the King made haste and sent messengers mounted upon horses, to call the men of the land that they might do battle with Orestes and his comrade. But while he was yet sending them there appeared in the air above his head the Goddess Athené, who spake, saying, " Cease, King Thoas, from pursuing this man and his companions; for he hath come hither on this errand by the command of Apollo; and I have persuaded Poseidon that he make the sea smooth for him to depart."

And King Thoas answered, " It shall be as thou wilt, O goddess; and though Orestes hath borne away his sister and the image, I dismiss my anger, for who can fight against the Gods?"

So Orestes departed and came to his own country and dwelt in peace, being set free from his madness, according to the word of Apollo.

THE STORY OF THE PERSIANS, OR THE BATTLE OF SALAMIS.

Xerxes, King of Persia, made war against the men of Greece, being desirous to have them for his servants. For being a man of a haughty soul, he thought to make the whole world subject to him; and against the men of Greece he had especial wrath, seeing that in the days of King Darius his father the Persians had fled before them. Wherefore he gathered together a great army from all parts of his dominions, every tribe and nation that there was in the whole land of the East, Indians, and Arabs, and such as dwelt in the plain country of Asia, having waggons for their houses, and Egyptians, and men from the upper parts of Libya. But the chief strength of his army was of the Medes and Persians, that were his own people. And for sailors he had Phœnicians, dwellers in

Tyre and Sidon, and in the coasts thereof. Also many Greeks with him, such as inhabited the cities of Asia that are near to the Greek sea, and the islands which are neighbours to them. But these loved him not, hating to fight against their brethren, but were constrained to join with him by fear. And when these were gathered together, being as the sand that is on the seashore for multitude, he marched into the land of Greece; and the ships also, being in number a thousand and more, sailed along as near as might be to the army, that there might be no escape for the Greeks either by land or sea.

But when the King had been gone now many days, and there came no tidings of him and the army, the old men, counsellors and princes, to whom had been committed the care of the realm while he should be absent, were gathered together before the palace in Susa, the royal city. Not a little troubled were they in mind, for the whole strength of the land was gone to the war. "Invincible," they said, "is the host of the Persians, and the people is valiant; but yet what man that is mortal can escape from

OR THE BATTLE OF SALAMIS. 221

the craft of the Gods, when they lure him to his ruin? Who is so nimble of foot that he can spring out of the net which they lay for his feet? Now of old the Persians fought ever upon the land, but now have they ventured where the waves of the sea grow white with the wind; and my heart is sore afraid, lest there come evil news that the city of Susa is emptied of her men. Then should there be heard great wailing of women; and the fine linen of the daughters of Persia, who even now sit at home alone, would be rent for grief. But come, let us sit and take counsel together, for our need is sore, and reckon the chances which of the two hath prevailed—the Persian bow or the spear of Greece."

But while they thus spake together there came forth to them from within the palace Queen Atossa, borne in a litter. And the old men did obeisance to her, bowing their heads to the ground. (Now Queen Atossa had been wife to Darius, and was the mother of King Xerxes.) And when they had greeted her, she told them for what cause she had come forth from the palace, for that she feared greatly lest the wealth which King Darius had gathered together should be overset. "For I know not," she said, "which is the worse thing, store of wealth without manhood, or lack of riches to them that are strong."

Then the old men bade her speak on, for that they would give her with all willingness such counsel as they could. After this the Queen set forth the matter to them, saying—

"I have been visited with many dreams and visions of the night since the day when King Xerxes my son departed hence with his army, purposing to subdue the men of Greece; but never have I seen vision so clear as that which I beheld in this night that is last past. I saw two women clothed with fair garments, the one being clad in Persian apparel, and the other in that which Grecian women used to wear. Very tall were they, above the stature of women in these days, and fair, so that no man might blame their beauty. Sisters also were they of the same race; but the one dwelt in the land of the Greeks, and the other in the land of Asia. Between these two there arose a strife; and my son took and soothed them, and would have yoked them to his chariot. Then she that wore the Persian garb was quiet and obedient to the bit; but the other fought against him, and tare with her hands the trappings of the chariot, and brake the yoke in the midst, so that my son fell upon the ground; and when he was fallen, lo! his father Darius stood over him, pitying him. This was my dream; and when I had risen and washed my hands in the running stream, I went to the altar, that I might offer incense to the Gods that avert evil from men; and there I saw an eagle fleeing to the altar of Phœbus, and a kite pursued after him, and flew upon him, and tare his head with his claws; nor did the eagle aught but yield himself up to his adversary. Now these are fearful things for me to see and also for you to hear. But remember that if my son shall prosper, all men will do him honour; and if he shall fail, yet shall he give account to no man, but be still ruler of this land."

To this the chief of the old men made answer, "O lady, we would counsel thee first to ask the Gods that they turn away all evils, and bring to pass all that is good; and next to make offerings to Earth and to the dead, and specially to thy husband King Darius, whom thou sawest in visions of the night, that he may send blessings from below to thy son, and turn away all trouble into darkness and nothingness."

"This will I do," said the Queen, "so soon as I shall have gone back to the palace. But first I would hear certain things of you. Tell me, my friends, in what land is this Athens of which they speak?"

"It is far to the west," the old men made reply, "towards the setting of the sun."

"And why did my son seek to subdue this city?"

"Because he knew that if he prevailed against it all Greece should be subject unto him."

"Hath it, then, so many men that draw the sword?"

"Such an army it hath as hath wrought great damage to the Medes."

"And hath it aught else, as wealth sufficient?"

"There is a spring of silver, a treasure hid in their earth."

"Do the men make war with bows?"

"Not so; they have spears for close fighting and shields."

"And who is master of their army?"

"They are not slaves or subjects to any man."

"How, then, can they abide the onset of the Persians?"

"Nay, but so well they abide it that they slew a great army of King Darius."

"What thou sayest is ill to hear for the mothers of them that are gone."

And when the Queen had thus spoken, the counsellors espied a man of Persia running to them with all speed, and knew that he bare tidings from the hosts, whether good or evil. And when the man was come, he cried out, "O land of Persia, abode of proud wealth, how are thy riches destroyed, and the flower of thy strength perished! 'Tis an ill task to bring such tidings, yet I am constrained to tell all our trouble. O men of Persia, the whole army of our land hath perished."

Then the old men cried out, bewailing themselves that they had lived to see this day. And the messenger told them how he had himself seen this great trouble befall the Persians, and had not heard it from others, and that it was at Salamis that the army had perished, and the city of Athens that had been chief among their enemies, the old men breaking in upon his story as he spake with their lamentations. But after a while the Queen Atossa stood forward, saying, "For a while I was dumb, for the trouble that I heard suffered me not to speak. But we must bear what the Gods send. Tell me, therefore, who is yet alive? and for whom must we make lamentation?"

"Know, O Queen," said the messenger, "that thy son, King Xerxes, is yet alive."

And the Queen cried, "What thou sayest is as light after darkness to me; but say on."

And when the messenger had told the names of many chiefs that had perished, the Queen said, "Come, let us hear the whole matter from the beginning. How many in number were the ships of the Greeks that they dared to meet the Persians in battle array?"

Then the man made reply, "In numbers, indeed, they might not compare with us; for the Greeks had three hundred ships in all, and ten besides that were chosen for their swiftness; but King Xerxes, as thou knowest, had a thousand, and of ships excelling in speed two hundred and seven. Of a truth, we wanted not for strength; but some God hath destroyed our host, weighing us against our enemies in deceitful balances."

And the Queen made reply, "'Tis even so: the Gods preserve the city of Pallas."

"Yea," said the man, "Athens is safe, though it be laid waste with fire; for the city that hath true men hath a sure defence."

"But say," said the Queen, "who began this battle of ships? Did the Greeks begin, or my son, trusting in the greatness of his host?"

Then the messenger answered, "Some evil demon set on foot all this trouble. For there came a man from the army of the Athenians to King Xerxes, saying that when night should come the Greeks would not abide in their place, but, taking with haste to their ships, would fly as best they could, and so save their lives. And he straightway, not knowing that the man lied, and that the Gods were jealous of him, made a proclamation to all the captains,

"So soon as the sun be set upon the earth and the heavens dark, order your ships in three companies, and keep the channels this way and that, and compass about the whole island of Salamis; for if by any means the Greeks escape, know that ye shall pay your lives for their lives.' This commandment did he give in his pride, not knowing what should come to pass. Whereupon all the people in due order made provision of meat and fitted their oars to the rowlocks; and when night was come, every man-at-arms embarked upon the ships. And the word of the command passed from line to line, and they sailed each to his appointed place. They then watched the channels all the night, yet nowhere was there seen any stir among the Greeks as of men that would fly by stealth. And when the fiery chariot of the Sun was seen in heaven, the Greeks set up with one accord a great shout, to which the echo from the rocks of the island made reply; and the Persians were troubled, knowing that they had been deceived, for the Greeks shouted not as men that were afraid. And after this there came the voice of a trumpet exceeding loud, and then, when the word was given, the dash of many oars that struck the water together, and, clearly heard above all, the sound of many voices, saying, ' RISE, CHILDREN OF THE GREEKS; SET FREE YOUR COUNTRY AND YOUR CHILDREN AND YOUR WIVES, AND THE HOUSES OF YOUR GODS, AND THE SEPULCHRES OF YOUR FOREFATHERS. NOW MUST YE FIGHT FOR ALL THAT YE HOLD DEAR.' And from us there came a great tumult of Persian speech, and the battle began, ship striking against ship. And a ship of the Greeks led the way, breaking off all the forepart of a ship of Phœnicia. For a while, indeed, the Persian fleet bare up; but seeing that there were many crowded together in narrow space, and that they could not help one another, they began to smite their prows together, and to break the oars one of the other. And the ships of the Greeks in a circle round about them drave against them right skilfully; and many hulls were overset, till a man could not see the sea, so full was it of wrecks and of bodies of dead men, with which also all the shores and rocks were filled. Then did all the fleet of the Persians take to flight without order, and our enemies with oars and pieces of wreck smote us, as men smite tunnies or a shoal of other fish; and there went up a dreadful cry, till the darkness fell and they ceased from pursuing. But all the evils that befell us I could not tell, no, not in ten days; only be sure of this, that never before in one day died such a multitude of men."

Then the Queen said, " 'Tis surely a great sea of troubles that hath broken upon our race."

But the messenger made reply, " Listen yet again, for I have yet more to tell. There is an island over against Salamis, small, not easy of approach to ships. Hither the King, thy son, sent the chosen men of his army, being in the vigour of their age, and noble of birth, and faithful to himself. For it was in his mind that they should slay such of the Greeks as should seek to save themselves out of the ships, and should help any of his own people that might be in need. But he judged ill of what should come to pass. For when the ships of the Greeks had prevailed as I have said, certain of their host clad themselves in arms, and leapt out of the ships on to the island, which they circled about so that the Persians knew not whither they should turn. And many were smitten down with stones, and many with arrows, till at the last the men of Greece, making an onslaught together, slew them with their swords so that there was not a man left alive. Which thing when the King beheld, for he sat on a hill nigh unto the shore of the sea, whence he could regard the whole army, he uttered a great cry, and rent his garments, and bade his army that was on the land fly with all speed."

And when the Queen heard these things she said, "O my son, ill hast thou avenged thyself on this city of Athens! But tell me, messenger, what befell them that escaped from the battle?"

"As for the ships," he said, "O Queen, such as perished not in the bay fled without order, the wind favouring them. But of the army many indeed perished of thirst in the land of Bœotia, and the rest departed with all speed through the land of Phocis and the coasts of Doris till we came to the region of Thessaly, being in sore straits for food. And here also many perished of hunger and thirst; but such as were left came into the land of Macedonia, and thence to the coasts of Thrace, even to the great river of Strymon. And there the Gods caused that there should be a frost out of season, so that the river was covered with ice in one night; which marvel when we beheld we worshipped the Gods, yea, such as had said before in their hearts that there were no Gods. And when our prayers were ended we crossed over; and with such as crossed before the sun was risen high upon the earth, it was well; for as the day grew towards noon, the ice was melted in the midst of the river, and the people fell through, one upon the other, and perished miserably, so that he might be counted happiest that died most speedily. But such as remained fled across the plains of Thrace with much toil and trouble, and are now come to our homes, being but a very few out of many."

Then said the Queen, "Truly my dream is fulfilled to the utmost. But now let us do what we may. For the past no man may change; but for the future we may take thought. Wherefore I will offer incense to the Gods and to the dead; and do you take faithful counsel together, and if the King my son should come before I be returned, comfort him and bring him to the palace, lest a yet worse thing befall us."

Then the Queen departed; and the old men made lamentation for the dead, and bewailed themselves for the trouble that had befallen the land of Persia. But after a while she returned, walking on her feet and in sober array, for she would put away all pride and pomp, knowing that the Gods were wroth with the land and its rulers. And she brought with her such things as men are wont to offer to the dead—milk and honey, and pure water from a fountain, and pure juice of a wild vine; also the fruit of the olive, and garlands of flowers; and she bade the old men sing a hymn to the dead, and call up the spirit of King Darius, while she offered her offerings to them that bear rule in hell.

So the old men chanted their hymn. To Earth they cried and to Hermes that they would send up the spirit of King Darius; also to the King himself they cried, that he would come and give them counsel in their need.

And after a while the spirit of the King rose

up from his sepulchre, having a royal crown upon his head, and a purple robe about him, and sandals of saffron upon his feet. And the spirit spake, saying, "What trouble is this that seemeth to have come upon the land? For my wife standeth near to my tomb with offerings; and ye have called me with the cries that raise the dead. Of a truth this is a hard journey to take; for they that bear rule below are more ready to take than to give back. Yet am I come, for I have power among them. Yet hasten, for my time is short. Tell me, what trouble hath come upon the land of Persia?"

But the old men could not answer him for fear. Whereupon he turned him to the Queen, and said, "My wife that was in time past, cease awhile from these lamentations and tell me what hath befallen this land."

And when she had told him all, he said, "Truly the Gods have brought speedy fulfilment to the oracles, which I had hoped might yet be delayed for many years. But what madness was this in Xerxes my son! Much do I fear lest our wealth be the prey of the spoiler."

Then the Queen made reply, "O my lord,

Xerxes hath been taught by evil counsellors; for they told him that thou didst win great wealth for thy country by thy spear, but that he sat idly at home; wherefore he planned this thing that hath now had so ill an end."

With this the old men, taking heart, would know of the King what counsel he gave them for the time to come. And he said, "Take heed that ye make not war again upon these men of Greece." And when they doubted whether they might not yet prevail, he said, "Listen, for ye know not yet all that shall be. When the King, my son, departed, he took not with him his whole army, but left behind him many chosen men of war in the land of Bœotia by the river Æsopus. And for these there is a grievous fate in store. For they shall suffer punishment for all that they have done against Gods and men, seeing that they spared not the temples of the Gods, but threw down their altars, and brake their images in pieces. Wherefore they shall perish miserably, for the spear of the Greeks shall slay them in the land of Platæa. For the Gods will not that a man should have thoughts that are above the measure of a man. Also full-flowered insolence groweth to the fruit of destructions, and men reap from it a harvest of many tears. Do ye then bear Athens and the land of Greece in mind, and let no man, despising what is his and coveting another man's goods, so bring great wealth to ruin. For Zeus is ever ready to punish them that think more highly than they ought to think, and taketh a stern account. Wherefore do ye instruct the King with counsels that he cease to sin against the Gods in the pride of his heart. And do thou that art his mother go to thy house, and take from it such apparel as is seemly, and go to meet thy son, for the many rents that he hath made for grief gape in his garments about him. Comfort him also with gentle words; for I know that 'tis thy voice only that he will hear. And to you old men, farewell; and live happily while ye may, for there is no profit of wealth in the grave whither ye go."

And with these words the spirit of King Darius departed.

THE STORY OF ION.

In the temple of Apollo at Delphi there dwelt a fair youth, whose name was Ion. Tall he was and comely, like to the son of a King, but of his birth no man knew anything; for he had been laid, being yet a babe, at the door of the temple, and the priestess had brought him up for her son. So he had served the God from a child, being fed from the altar and from the gifts of the strangers that were wont to resort to the place. Now it was the lad's custom to rise early in the morning and to sweep the temple with boughs of bay, and to sprinkle it with water from the fountain of Castalia. Also he was wont to keep the birds from the temple— for they would come from the woods of Parnassus hard by, eagles, and swans, and others— lest they should settle on the pinnacles or defile the altar with their prey. And for this end he carried arrows and a bow, slaying the birds if need was, but rather seeking to frighten them away, for he knew that some carried messages from the Gods to mortal men, and warned them of things to come, even as did Apollo that was his master.

Now it befell on a day, when he had done his office in the temple, that there drew near to the doors a company of women. Maidens they were from the land of Attica, and they had come with Creüsa, who was Queen of the country. And first they marvelled at the graved work that was on the doors and in the porch, for some cunning workmen had wrought thereon Hercules slaying the great dragon of Lerna, and Iolaüs standing with a torch to sear that which he cut with his knife. Also Bellerophon was to be seen on a horse with wings, slaying the Chimæra; and Pallas fighting against the Sons of Earth, with the thunderbolt of her father Zeus and the shield of the Gorgon head. And when they had made an end of seeing these things came the Queen Creüsa herself and had speech with Ion. And she told him that she was the daughter of Erechtheus, King of Athens, and that she was married to Xuthus, a Prince from the island of Pelops. And when Ion would know how it had come to pass that Xuthus, being a stranger and a foreigner, had received her that was a Princess of the land in marriage, she said that the Prince had fought for the men of Athens against the land of Euboea, and had subdued it, and so had won for himself this reward. Also when the youth would know for what end she had come to the oracles of Delphi, she said that she had come because having been long married she was yet childless, and that her husband also was with her, and that he was even then making inquiry about this same matter in the cave of Trophonius. For there also was an oracle giving answers to men about things to come. Then the Queen asked Ion of his estate, and heard from him that the priestess of Apollo had brought him up, having found him laid at the door of the temple.

After these things came King Xuthus himself, who, after he had greeted the Queen, said that Trophonius would not indeed go before the answer of Apollo, yet promised this, that he should not go to his home childless. So the two went together into the shrine that they might inquire yet further of the matter; and Ion abode without, meditating much on the things which these strangers had said.

But after a while the King came forth in great joy, and when he saw the youth Ion standing without the shrine, he caught him by the hand, and would have thrown his arms about him, but the youth drew back, thinking that the God had smitten him with madness, and even would have drawn his bow against him. Then the King set forth to him the answer that Apollo had given him. For the God had said, "Thou art not childless as thou thinkest, but the father of a fair son. And thy son is he whom first thou shalt meet going forth from my shrine." "And now," said the King, "thou art he whom first I meet coming forth, and I claim thee to be my son." And when Ion would know how this might be, the King said that in days past, before he had married the Princess Creüsa, being young and foolish, he had taken to wife a maiden of low degree in this very city of Delphi, and that if she had borne him a son—for that he knew not, having left her long since—the child would bear such age as Ion. And when Ion heard this he was glad, for he had feared lest haply he should be found to be the son of some slave. Only he said to himself, "O my dear mother, shall I ever see thee? For now do I long more than ever to look upon thee; but haply thou art dead and this may never be."

And the maidens of Athens standing by heard the talk between the two, and said, "It is well for the people that the royal house should prosper. Yet it had pleased us well that our lady the Queen should have hope of offspring, and that the house of Erechtheus should not be left without an heir."

Then said the King to Ion, "My son, it is well both with thee and me, for I have found that which I most desired and thou also. And as to that which thou now sayest about thy mother, haply, if only we have patience, this also shall be as thou wouldst have it. But now I would have thee leave the temple of Apollo and this thy subsistence of alms, and come with me to the great city of Athens, where thou shalt have great wealth, and in due time this sceptre that I hold. But why art thou silent and castest thine eyes to the ground? Suddenly art thou changed from joy to sorrow, and the heart of thy father misgiveth him."

Then spoke Ion, saying, "My father, the aspect of many things changeth according as a man seeth them, whether it be near or afar off. Right glad was I to find a father in thee; but as to what else thou sayest, hearken to me. Men say that the Athenians are a people that have dwelt in the land from the beginning. Wherefore I shall have among them a double reproach, being both basely born and also a foreigner. And if I come to high place in the state, they that are beneath me shall hate me, seeing that men love not those that are above them. Also those that are of high account among the citizens shall have much jealousy against me, for such men have ever great enmity against their rivals. Think also of thy house, how matters shall stand there. For before, thy wife the Queen shared with thee this reproach of childlessness, but now will she stand alone and bear her sorrow by herself. How then shall she not hate me when she seeth me at thy right hand? And so shalt thou either for love of her go back from what thou hast promised to me, or else, seeking my profit, shalt trouble thine own house. For thou knowest what deadly deeds with the sword and with poison women holding themselves to be wronged have wrought against their husbands. And of a truth, my father, I hold that thy wife, seeing that she groweth old without hope of children, is most miserable among women. And then as to kingship, I count that this is more pleasant to regard from afar than to possess; for how can he be happy who liveth in daily fear of death? And if thou sayest that great store of wealth outweigheth all other things, and that it is pleasant to be rich, I hold otherwise. I would have neither poverty nor riches, but to live quietly and without trouble. For listen, my father, to the good things that I have had in this place—that which all men count dear, even leisure; and such labour as I did, not toilsome, and to be free from all ill company, and to be constant in prayers to the Gods, or in talk with men, ever consorting with new company among such as came to inquire of the god. Surely, my father, this life is better than that which thou promisest to me."

"My son," the King made answer, "learn to take the good which the Gods have provided for thee. First, then, I will bring thee to the feast which I purpose to hold in this place as though thou wert a stranger. And afterwards I will take thee to the city of Athens, yet not declaring at the first thy birth, for I would not vex my wife with my good luck, seeing that she is yet childless. Only in time I will work with her that thou shalt bear rule in the land with her good will. And now call such of thy friends as thou wilt to the feast, for thou must even bid farewell to this city of Delphi."

And Ion made answer, "Let it be so; only if I find not my mother, my life is nothing worth."

And to the maidens the King said, "Take heed that ye keep silence on these matters, or ye shall surely die."

But they were much troubled in heart for their mistress that she should be childless, while the King her husband had found a son. Also they doubted much whether they should not tell the Queen the things which they had heard.

And now there was seen to come near to the

shrine an old man who had in days past been servant to King Erechtheus; and when the Queen saw him, she reached her hand to him, and helped him to climb the steps of the temple, for he was very feeble with age. And when he was come to the top, the Queen turned her to the maidens that stood by and inquired of them whether they knew aught of the answer which the God had given to her husband in the matter of his childlessness. But they were loath to make answer, remembering that the King had bidden them to be silent under pain of death; but at the last, for the thing pleased them not, both for pity of their mistress and also for hatred that a stranger should be King in Athens, they said, "O lady, thou must never hold a child in thy arms or nurse a babe at thy breast." And when the old man asked—for the Queen was distraught with grief—whether the King also shared this trouble, they said, "Not so, old man; to him Apollo giveth a son."

"How so?" said he; "is this son yet to be born, or doth he live already?"

"He is a youth full grown. For the God

said, 'He whom thou shalt first meet, coming forth from this shrine, is thy son.' And know, lady, that this youth is he who is wont to serve in this shrine, with whom thou talkedst at the first. But more than this I know not; only that thy husband is gone without thy knowledge to hold a great feast, and that the lad sitteth thereat in much honour."

And when the old man heard these things he waxed wroth and said, "Lady, there is treachery in this matter. We are betrayed by thy husband, and of fixed purpose set at naught, that he may drive us out of the house of thy father, King Erechtheus. And this I say not because I hate thy husband, but that I love thee more. Hearken, then, to my words. He came a stranger to the city of Athens, and took thee to wife, and had with thee the inheritance of thy father's kingdom; and when he found thee childless, he was not content to bear this reproach with thee, but wedded secretly some slave woman, and gave the child whom she bare to him to some citizen of Delphi to rear for him. And the child grew up, as thou knowest, a minister in the temple of Apollo. And when thy husband

THE STORY OF ION.

knew that he was come to full age he devised this device that thou and he should come to this place, and make inquiry of the god, whether there might be any remedy for thy childlessness. And now thou wilt suffer the foulest wrong, for he will bring this son of a bondwoman to be lord in thy house. Wherefore I give thee this counsel. Devise some device, and be it with the sword or with poison, or with whatever thou wilt, slay thy husband and his son, or they shall surely slay thee. For if thou spare them thou wilt surely die. For if there be two enemies under one roof, it must needs be that the one perish. And now, if thou wilt, I will do this deed for thee, and slay them at the feast which he prepareth; for I have had sustenance in the house of thy father to this day, for which I would fain make this return."

Then the Queen and the old man talked together about the matter. And when he would have had her slay her husband, she refused, saying that she could not do the deed, for that she thought of the time when he was faithful and loving to her. But when he would have her execute vengeance on the youth, she consented. Only she doubted how this might be done. Then the old man cried, "Arm thine attendants with the sword and slay him."

"Aye," said the Queen, "and I would lead them myself; but where shall I slay him?"

"Slay him," said the old man, "in the tent where he feasteth his friends."

"Nay," answered the Queen, "the deed would be too manifest; the hands also of slaves are ever feeble."

Then the old man cried in a rage, "I see thou playest the coward. Take counsel for thyself."

Then said the Queen, "I have a plan in my heart that is both crafty and sure. Listen now, and I will unfold it to thee. Thou knowest how in time past the Giants that were the sons of Earth made war against the Gods in the plain of Phlegra; and that Earth, seeking to help her children, brought forth the Gorgon; and that Pallas, the daughter of Zeus, slew the monster. Know then that Pallas gave to Ericthonius, who was the first King of the land of Attica, being sprung from the earth, two drops of the blood of the Gorgon, whereof the one hath the power to kill whomsoever it shall touch, and the other to heal all manner of diseases. And these she shut in gold to keep them; and Ericthonius gave them to King Erechtheus my father, and he, when he died, gave them to me. And I carry them in a bracelet on my wrist. And thou shalt take the one that worketh death, and with it thou shalt slay this youth."

" 'Tis well thought," the old man made answer; " but where shall I do the deed?"

" In Athens," said the Queen, "when he shall have come to my house."

But the old man said, " That is not well; for thou wilt have the repute of the deed, even if thou slay him not. Slay him rather in this place, where thou shalt be more likely to deceive thy husband, for it must not be that he know it."

When the Queen heard this she said, " Hear, then, what thou must do. Go to the place where my husband maketh a sacrifice and a feast following. And when the guests are even now ready to cease from their feasting and make libations to the Gods, drop his drop of death into the cup of him who would lord it over my house. Of a surety if it pass his throat he shall never come to the city of Athens."

So the old man went on his errand, and as he went he said to himself, "Old foot of mine, do this thy business as though thou wert young. Thou hast to help the house of thy master against an enemy. Let them that are happy talk of piety; he that would work his adversary woe must take no account of laws."

But meanwhile Xuthus had bidden the youth Ion have a care for the feast, for that he himself had yet sacrifice to make, at which he might haply tarry long time. Wherefore Ion set up a great tent on poles, looking neither wholly to the south nor to the west, but between the two. And the tent he made foursquare, being of a hundred feet each way, for he purposed to call the whole people of Delphi to the feast. Then he took curtains from the treasure-house to cover it within, very marvellous to behold; for on them was wrought the Heaven with all the gathering of the stars, and the Sun driving his chariot to the west, and dark-robed Night, with the stars following her, the Pleiades, and Orion with his sword, and the Bear turning about the Pole, and the bright circle of the Moon; and on the other side the Morning chasing the stars. Also there were tapestries from foreign land, ships fighting with ships, and strange shapes, half men half beasts, and the hunting of stags and lions.

But in the midst of the tent great bowls were set for wine; and a herald bade all the men of Delphi to the feast. But when they had had enough of eating and drinking, the old man, the servant of the Queen, came forward; and all men laughed to see him how busy he was. For he took the water that should have been mixed with the wine and used it for the washing of hands, and burnt the incense, and took upon himself the ordering of the cups. And after a while he said, "Take away those cups, and bring greater that we may be merry." So they brought great cups of gold and silver. And the old man took one that was more beautiful than the rest, and filled it to the brim and gave it to the youth Ion, as though he would do him great honour; but he dropped into it the deadly drop. Only no man saw the thing that he did. But when they were all about to drink, some one spake an evil word to his neighbour, and Ion heard it, and having full knowledge of augury, held it to be of ill omen, and bade them fill another bowl; and that every one should pour out upon the ground that which was in his cup. And on this there came down a flight of doves, for such dwelt in the temple of Apollo without fear, and sipped of the wine that had been poured forth. And all the rest drank and suffered no harm; but that which had settled where the youth Ion had poured out from his cup shook and reeled and screamed aloud, and so died, being sorely rent with the pangs of death. And when the youth saw this he cried, "Who is it that hath plotted my death? Tell me, old man, for thou gavest me the cup." And he leapt over the table and laid hands on him. And at last the old man, being sorely pressed, unfolded the whole matter. Then Ion gathered all the Princes of Delphi together, and told them that the strange woman, the daughter of Erechtheus, had plotted his death by poison. And the sentence of the Princes was that she should be cast down from the rock on which their city was built, because she had sought to slay with poison the minister of the god.

Then one who had seen the whole matter

THE STORY OF ION.

from the beginning to the end, ran with all speed and told it to the Queen; and she, when she heard it, and that the officers of the people were coming to lay hands on her, fled to the altar of Apollo, and sat upon it in the place whereon the sacrifice was laid; for they that flee to the altar are sacred, and it is a sin against the god if any man touch them. But in a short space came Ion with a troop of armed men, breathing out threats and fury against the Queen. And when he saw her he said, "What a viper is this that thou hast brought forth, land of Attica! Worse is she than the drop of Gorgon's blood wherewith she would have slain me. Seize her that she may be thrown from the rock. 'Tis well for me that I set not foot in her house in Athens; for then had she caught me in a net, and I had surely died. But now the altar of Apollo shall not save her."

And he bade the men drag her from the holy place. But even as he spake came in the Pythia, the priestess. And when Ion had greeted her, asking her whether she knew how this woman had sought to slay him, she answered that she knew it, but that he too was fierce above measure, and that he must not defile with blood the house whereto he went in the city of Athens. And when he was loath to listen to her, she said, "Seest thou this that I hold in my hand?" Now what she held was a basket with tufts of wool about it. "This is that in which I found thee, long ago, a new-born babe. And Apollo hath laid it upon me not to say aught of this before, but now to give it into thy hands. Take it, therefore, for the swaddling clothes wherein thou wast wrapped are within, and find out for thyself of what race thou art. And now, farewell; for I love thee as a mother loveth her child."

Then Ion said to himself, "This is a sorrowful thing to see, this basket in which my mother laid me long since, putting me away from her in secret, so that I have grown up as one without a name in this temple. The god hath dealt kindly with me, yet hath my fortune and the fortune of my mother been but ill. And what if I find that I am the son of some bondwoman. It was better to know nought than to know this. But I may not fight against the will of the

god; wherefore I will open it and hear my past whatever it be."

So he opened the basket, and marvelled that it was not wasted with time, and that there was no decay upon that which was within. But when the Queen saw the basket, she knew it, and leapt from where she sat upon the altar, and told him all that was in her heart, that in time past, before she was wedded to King Xuthus, she had borne a son to Apollo, and had laid the babe in this basket, and with him swaddling clothes of things which she had woven with her own hands, and "Thou," she said, "art my son, whom I see after this long time."

And when the young man doubted whether this was so, the Queen told him the pattern of the clothes; that there was one which she had woven being yet a girl, not finished with skill, but like rather to the task of one that learns, and that there was wrought upon it the head of the Gorgon, and that it was fringed about with snakes, like to Pallas's shield, the ægis. Also she said that there were necklaces wrought like to the scales of a snake, and a wreath of olive besides, as befitted the child of a daughter of Athens.

Then Ion knew that the Queen was his mother; yet was he sore perplexed, for the god had given him as a son to King Xuthus, nor did he doubt but that the god ever speaketh that which is true. Then he said that he would himself inquire of Apollo. But as he turned to go, lo! a great brightness in the air, and the shape as of one of the dwellers in heaven. And when he was afraid, and would have fled with the Queen, there came a voice, saying, "Flee not, for I am a friend and not an enemy. I am Pallas, and I come from King Apollo with a message to this youth and to the Queen. To Ion he saith, 'Thou art my son, whom this woman bare to me in time past.' And to the Queen, 'Take this thy son with thee to the city of Athens, and set him on the throne of thy father, for it is meet that he, being of the race of Erechtheus, should sit thereon. And know that he shall become a great nation, and that his children in time to come shall dwell in the islands of the sea, and in the lands that border thereon, and that they shall be called Ionians after his name. Know also that thou shalt bear children to Xuthus—Dorus and Æolus—and that these also shall become fathers of nations.'"

And when the goddess had thus spoken she departed; and the two, Ion and Queen Creüsa, with King Xuthus also, went to their home in great joy and peace.